THE MEDIEVAL CASTLE

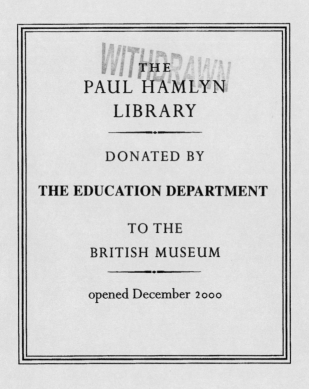

THEN AND THERE SERIES
GENERAL EDITOR
MARJORIE REEVES, M.A., PH.D.

The Medieval Castle

MARJORIE REEVES, M.A., PH.D.

Illustrated from contemporary sources by

H. C. McBEATH

LONGMAN

LONGMAN GROUP LIMITED
Longman House
Burnt Mill, Harlow, Essex, CM20 2JE, England

First published 1963
Twelfth impression 1982

ISBN 0 582 20392 9

FOR ANNE REEVES

ACKNOWLEDGMENTS

Thanks are due to Dr R. Harvey for making the translations
from the poem *Guillaume le Marechal* and Mrs Booth for
selecting the poem on p. 49.

We should also like to acknowledge the assistance received
from the following books in the preparation of a number of
line drawings: Hamilton-Thompson: *Military Architechture
During the Middle Ages* (O.U.P.) and S. Toy: *The Castles of
Great Britain* (Heineman).

*Printed in Hong Kong by
Wing Tai Cheung Printing Co Ltd*

CONTENTS

TO THE READER

History is all round us, if we use our eyes. England was once a land of many castles and, though some have vanished completely, you can still detect many as you travel around the country. Sometimes nothing is left but a high grass mound or a bit of broken wall; sometimes you can still see the castle standing, but all in ruins, with roofless hall and tottering towers; sometimes the castle has been modernized into a more comfortable place to live in. When you look at any of these you must try to imagine what life was like in the days when castles were strong fortresses as well as houses, when castle-dwellers watched for enemies from their walls and besieging armies used all their cunning to find a way of breaking in. To have lived in a castle then must have been uncomfortable but exciting.

The First Castle-builders

If you had been William the Conqueror just after the Norman Conquest of England, what would you have thought was the most important thing to do first? There might be several answers to that question, but in fact one of the first things William and his Norman barons thought about was CASTLES. A strong castle with good *fortifications*[1] was like a hedgehog with its bristles out: it was hard to get near it, it was harder still to overcome it. William's Norman followers could shut themselves up safely inside, protected from their Anglo-Saxon enemies, and when they chose, sally forth on war expeditions all round the countryside. Soon after the Norman Conquest, therefore, England bristled with castles.

Many of these first castles were built in a great hurry: the Normans made them the quickest way they knew. Here they are building the first castle, immediately after winning the battle of Hastings, and they are building it at Hastings itself:

IVSSIT: VT FODERETVR: CASTELLVM AT HESTENGA

---

[1] You will find the meanings of words printed like *this* in the Glossary on page 100.

Can you see how they do it? The men are throwing up a great mound of earth which they call a *motte*. Round the foot of this there will be a deep ditch. On top of the motte they will build a strong wooden wall, called a *stockade* or *palisade*, and inside it probably a wooden tower or *keep*. On one side of the motte there will be a kind of yard with a stockade and perhaps a ditch and bank all round it. This is called a *bailey*. This was the common plan of many of the first castles in England. Some were built of stone instead of wood, but they nearly all had a motte and a bailey. So we call them motte-and-bailey castles. Now here is a plan of a very simple one:

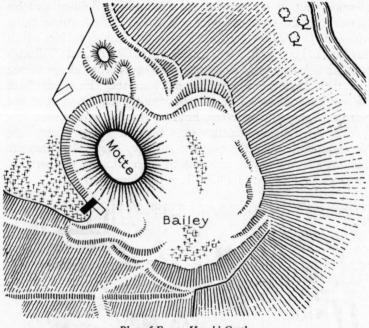

Plan of Ewyas Harold Castle

Sometimes they made two baileys, an outer and an inner one, and, very occasionally, two mottes. So, just to show you what different

2

shapes they could be, here is the plan of another motte-and-bailey castle.

Where would you place your castles in a newly-conquered country? Look at the maps carefully and try to discover some of the geographical reasons for the placing of Norman castles. (See inside front and back cover.) When a castle is placed in a strong position for defence or attack, we say it occupies a *strategic point*.

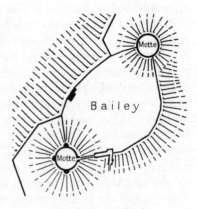

Plan of Lewes Castle

Now have you spotted the following:

(*a*) castles which guard the coast from foreign invasions. Why are these mostly in the south and east?

(*b*) castles which guard important rivers. Why were these necessary?

(*c*) castles guarding the Scottish and Welsh borders. You will easily think of the reasons for these.

As William the Conqueror marched to and fro in England crushing the rebellions of the English, he noted the good spots for castles and gave one or other of his barons the task of building and guarding them as his *castellans*. These were the royal castles: the barons in charge of them were only keepers of these castles for the King. But William also gave permission to many barons to build their own castles as well, especially in the dangerous parts of the country. Here they lived with their families, for in those unsafe days a Norman baron wanted his family inside a fortress.

The most famous of the royal castles was the White Tower which William started building at once to keep a tight hold on London. It is now the oldest part of the great Tower of London which stands beside the Thames, guarding the approach to London up the river. This was a stone castle from the beginning, built especially strong because it did not stand up high on a motte. William also had a stone castle built at Colchester, an important point at the head of the estuary of the river Colne, where Danish invaders might easily sail in. Here there had once been an important Roman town, so the castle could be placed inside the old Roman fortifications and the builders found plenty of Roman stone and tiles which they could re-use. The keep they built here was the largest in England: it measured 152 by 111 ft. and was originally four stories high. Its windows were narrow slits called *loops*, widening out (or *splayed*) inside. This meant that, while a defender inside could easily shoot an arrow out, it would be very difficult for the attacker from outside to hit him through the narrow slit. You can still see in the bottom two floors of this keep which are left standing, the way the builders put the Roman tiles in what is called a herring-bone pattern.

Another stone castle William built was at Exeter, after the people in Somerset and Devon had rebelled against him. Most other royal castles probably began by being earth-and-wood ones.

As William marched north to crush the rebellious people of Yorkshire, he picked out Warwick and Nottingham for two castles to mount guard over two important roads. At Warwick there was a useful bend in the river to protect the castle and at Nottingham a fine high ridge of land with steep sides. He put the Beaumont family in charge of Warwick and made William Peveril castellan of Nottingham. At York he ordered two castles to be built—one each side of the river Ouse—because the people were so discontented and dangerous. On the way back he stopped at Lincoln to order the building of a castle inside the old Roman fort which was up on a hill. Even so, they thought it necessary to throw up two mottes, instead of one, and destroyed many houses while building the castle. At the same time William had castles built at Huntingdon and Cambridge. On a later march north he ordered the constructtion of castles at Durham, Chester and Shrewsbury. You can still see what a splendid place the Normans chose at Durham: the river sweeps round in a great loop with steep banks, and right in this loop the castle and the cathedral were built side by side.

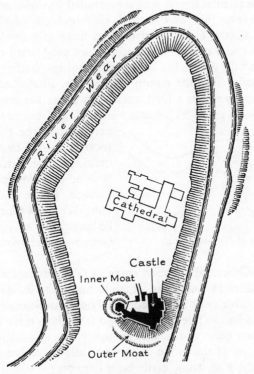

Site of Durham Castle

When he had conquered Hereward the Wake, the last of the English rebels, William built Ely castle to mount guard over the marshes where Hereward and his men had hidden. Other important royal castles which William ordered to be built were Bramber and Lewes in Sussex, Dover, Bristol, Gloucester, Rockingham, Stafford, Stamford, Pontefract.

William's barons were most energetic castle-builders. As soon as he permitted, off they went into the part of England where he had given them lands, with keen eyes searching out the lie of the land for the strongest points at which to place their castles. In the

5

west William FitzOsbern was commanded by William to build castles wherever they were needed. He found a wonderful site for Chepstow Castle. Here the river Wye flows into the wide river Severn, and so a castle garrison could not only guard the border against the wild Welsh, but also watch for ships, trading or invading, that sailed into the mouth of the river. FitzOsbern chose a place where there was a high, rocky cliff above the water, with a deep ravine to guard its landward side. He did not need a motte here, but at the highest and rockiest point he began to build his castle. Farther up the Wye he built Monmouth and Clifford Castle and, in the same Welsh border country, he built castles at Wigmore and Grosmont and rebuilt Ewyas Castle.

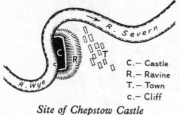

C.— Castle
R.— Ravine
T.— Town
c.— Cliff

Site of Chepstow Castle

But FitzOsbern also owned lands in Gloucestershire and here was very different country in which to find a site for a castle—no rocky cliffs over swift rivers, but low-lying water-meadows. So at Berkeley he had to pile up a motte 50 ft. high to make his castle. On it he built quite a small wooden tower with a wooden stockade round the top of the motte. This first little castle has now been buried in the huge stone castle built later on.

The King's half-brother, Robert of Mortain, was a second great castle-builder. He had the important task of seeing that no other invaders landed at Pevensey, where William had landed. The obvious place here for a castle was the ancient Roman fort which was guarded by the sea on two sides and by marshes on the other two. Robert made his castle in the south-east corner of the old fort, where the Roman walls formed two sides of it, while on the other two he had a ditch, bank and palisade. Berkhamstead was another important castle probably built by Robert of Mortain, with a motte 40 ft. high, ditched all round, and a bailey of $2\frac{2}{3}$ acres with a ditch and a bank encircling it. To make it very strong, there was a second outer ditch right round motte and bailey together. You can see this

6

in the plan on p. 12. Near Poole Harbour on the south coast, Robert found another key-place at Corfe which is the only gap in the Purbeck Hills, a line of hills guarding that piece of the coast. Anyone landing on the coast and marching inland would almost certainly come through this gap, so there Robert of Mortain planted his castle, on a hill in the midst of the gap, with two streams flowing round the foot of it.

Roger of Montgomery was one of William's earls who had his lands in two different parts of England. On the one side, as you can guess, he held lands on the Welsh border, for Montgomeryshire is named after him. He was also Earl of Shrewsbury and was made castellan of the royal castle there. This castle stands in a bend of the river Severn and 51 houses of the town were destroyed to make its motte and bailey. Roger Montgomery and his family also built other castles on the Welsh border, including one at Quarford on a bold bit of rock jutting out into the Severn and one at Montgomery. But away down in the south of England Roger also held lands at Arundel on the south coast. Here it was necessary to guard the mouth of the river Arun against invasion. Roger found a high platform on the right bank of the river where he threw up his motte. East and south it was defended by the steep banks; north and west he cut ditches for defence. On the motte he probably built a wooden tower and fortified it with a wooden palisade all round.

Roger's sons were also energetic castle-builders. One, called Roger the Poitevin, built Clitheroe Castle on a high motte of natural rock; another, Arnulf of Montgomery, found a splendid site for Pembroke Castle in south Wales, on a high cliff close to the sea.

One bishop was a noted castle-builder—Gundulf, Bishop of Rochester. He may have superintended the building of the stone keeps at the Tower of London and at Colchester. At Rochester his motte was placed within old Roman walls; it had a ditch on three sides and the river on the fourth. He even built a stone tower here, but this is not the great stone keep we see today.

Oxford stood at a strategic point on the river Thames, at a place

7

where important roads met. Here there was no convenient rocky headland, for there were nothing but water-meadows all round. So Robert d'Oilli, the chief baron here, threw up a huge motte of earth which you can still see. He probably fortified it with wooden palisades and towers and he seems to have built a small stone tower, a chapel and a wooden hall for the large garrison of knights he had there.

Farther north the castle-builders were just as busy, for they had to guard against Scots raiders, invaders from Ireland or Scandinavia and outlaws in the wild mountain country. William Peveril, castellan of the royal castle at Nottingham, found a wonderful place in the Pennines where he perched his own castle on the Peak, with great precipices all round it. Of course he needed on motte here and he probably built the first walls of stone becaues this was easier to get than wood in this rocky place.

Robert Marmion built Tamworth Castle on low-lying ground just where the rivers Tame and Anker met. Here, of course, he had to throw up a motte with a ditch all round it. The bailey, too, was raised on a triangular platform of earth. Farther north, Robert de Busli built the castle of Tickhill with a magnificent motte 75 ft. high and the Earl de Warenne that of Conisbrough on the river Don. Farther north again, William I gave Ilbert de Lacythe task of building a castle on the rocky hill of Pontefract, to keep watch over the road north and to guard Airedale. He probably palisaded the top of the hill and built a wooden tower.

In Yorkshire the greatest baron was Alan of Brittany. He placed his chief castle at a point where it could control the whole of Swaledale, in a bend of the river Swale where a rocky platform stands 150 ft. above the water. He called it Richmond (a name he brought from France) and built there a castle which was never attacked because it was so strong. On every side it was defended either by the river or by a steep drop. Other castles built to guard the northern dales were Knaresborough in Nidderdale, Middleham in Wensleydale, Barnard Castle in Teesdale.

Finally, as sentinels against the Scots, there were—besides Durham—Norham Castle, built by Ranulf Flambard, Bishop of

8

Durham; Newcastle on the Tyne, built by Robert, son of William I; Alnwick, built by the Percies; Bamburgh, right on the sea-shore to guard the north-east coast. On the west side, opposite Newcastle, stood the royal castle of Carlisle. Farther south the great baron, Hugh d'Avranches, was very busy. First, at Tutbury he raised a great mound on top of a rocky hill, with steep precipices on two sides, so that his castle had a fine position. Then he took charge of Chester castle and also helped his *vassal* Robert of Rhuddlan to build a strong castle at Rhuddlan itself.

Of course when we say that William I or Hugh d'Avranches built a castle, we do not mean that they took up spades themselves and bent their backs to the heavy work of throwing up these great mounds. They chose the position and then forced the conquered English living round about to build as they commanded. So everywhere in England Anglo-Saxon peasants toiled to pile up the mottes, to cut timber for the wooden towers, to drive in stakes for the stockades round the motte and bailey. Everywhere in England these castles looked out grimly and watchfully over the conquered people. This was a time of danger for the Normans: at any moment there might be another rebellion of the English; at any moment a Norman, hunting through the forest, might be shot from behind a tree. So the barons lived in the safety of their castles and many of their knights with them. Other knights were given lands where they built their own manor-houses, but still, as part of their service to their lord, they had to take their turn in garrisoning his castle. This was called castle-guard and meant that every so often a knight would spend three or four months on duty at the castle.

It must have been grim living in those first castles. They were not built to be comfortable, but to be safe. Many were on high draughty places where the winds whistled through the wooden walls. Building towers for defence came first, but as soon as they had time the lords usually built a wooden hall where their knights could eat and sleep. This was sometimes on top of the motte and sometimes in the bailey. Probably attached to it were a separate Great Chamber for the lord and his family and some small rooms (or *bowers*) for the women. Close by they would build a kitchen and, as soon as possible, a chapel. Workshops, stables, armoury, storerooms—all these followed, and so the castle grew.

The first Norman barons had to run up their castles quickly because they needed their protection. Wood was generally quicker and handier to use than stone, hence the wooden castles, though, as we have seen, in some places it was easier to build in stone from the beginning. But when his castle was besieged a Norman baron soon found out the weaknesses of wood. You could chop through wood where stone only blunted the axe. Worse still, wooden

Trematon Castle showing curtain and shell-keep

towers and walls could be set on fire and the castle destroyed this way. So within fifty years of the Norman Conquest, kings and barons were busy transforming wooden castles into stone ones.

In many cases the first thing they did was to build a stone wall round the bailey in place of the wooden stockade. This was called a *curtain* wall, or stone curtain. Next, they often carried this wall up the sides of the motte to join the stockade round the top. The obvious thing to do then was to replace the old wooden stockade by a stone wall all round the top of the motte. This made what is called a *shell-keep*. Where the motte was an artificial mound of earth the builders knew that it was unsafe to plant down a heavy stone tower on the top without allowing many years for the earth to settle down. So they sometimes left the wooden keep on the motte. Sometimes they filled in the space inside the shell-keep with wooden buildings to live in, placed round a central courtyard. You can see the plan of a shell-keep castle very clearly in this picture of a small castle in Cornwall, at Restormel. Remember that any wooden buildings there might have been have long since disappeared.

Restormel Castle

Sometimes, however, the castle-builder wanted a good strong stone tower and in this case he generally built a four-sided tower called a *rectangular* keep. This was usually built in the bailey because the firmer ground there would stand the heavy weight better than the loose earth of the motte. Some also went on to build strong stone gatehouses, either at the entrance to the bailey, or to the motte, or both.

Of course not all castles were built according to this pattern, nor were they built at the same rate. Some were turned into stone castles very quickly; others took more than a hundred years over the change. We can often detect the length of time taken by differences in the stone-work: where it is very rough it will usually be early, belonging to the time of King William I or II; where it is smooth and regular, it will be nearly a hundred years later (at least), belonging, perhaps, to the time of Henry II. You can see this very clearly if you go to Richmond Castle in Yorkshire, where the curtain wall and hall are of rough stone, built probably by its first lord, Alan of Brittany, before 1088, while on top of the hall, between 1170 and 1180, there was built a splendid square keep of smooth, cut stone. Can you see the difference in the stone-work in this picture?

Richmond Castle, Yorkshire

Thus the Normans built two kinds of stone keep—a shell-keep and a rectangular keep. First of all we will look at some of the shell-keeps. The most famous is that of Windsor Castle, built as early as the reign of William the Conqueror on top of a chalk mound, in a bend of the river Thames. The first shell-wall stood 15 ft. above the mound; it is still there, but inside it a later king, Henry II, built a much higher tower, so that, in the picture on p. 14, only the bottom piece is the old shell-keep. Windsor Castle stands up grandly from the river and is one of our most splendid round castles.

Here is a plan of Berkhamsted Castle in Hertfordshire with the shell-keep which was probably built by William the Conqueror's half-brother, Robert of Mortain. Notice

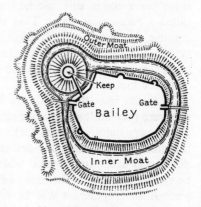

Plan of Berkhamsted Castle

that only one curtain wall runs up the motte to connect with the keep.

Robert Marmion built a shell-keep at Tamworth which was 25 ft. or more high and had walls 7 ft. thick. He cut a moat round the foot of the motte and encircled the bailey with a curtain wall. Then he carried the wall, as a causeway, over the moat and up the mound to join the keep. You can still see in the causeway wall the herring-bone pattern of stone-work which he built.

Arundel Castle, you remember, belonged to the Montgomery family. It was a member of this family, Robert of Belesme, who probably started the stone-building there. There were two baileys, one on each side of the motte, and round each a curtain wall was built. On top of the 70-ft. high motte, 9-ft. thick walls began to rise for the shell-keep. When this was finished a little later, it had a square, jutting-out tower with a well at the bottom and a chapel in it. As in other shell-keeps, you could climb up staircases in the thickness of the wall to the wall-walk which ran right round the top of it. If you visit Arundel today, you will be shown many magnificent buildings which are much later, but the motte and the old shell-keep still stand, a little distance from the rest. Can you spot them in this picture which shows the later castle as well?

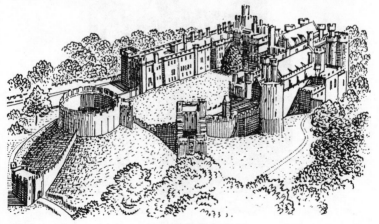

Arundel Castle today

13

The Keep, Windsor Castle

The Keep, Rochester Castle

The great rectangular keeps built by Norman kings and barons seem grimmer and stronger than the shell-keeps. Just as Windsor is the most famous shell-keep, so the White Tower of the Tower of London is the most famous rectangular keep. It rises to 90 ft. and the walls are 12 to 15 ft. thick. Try to visit it for yourself one day and remember to notice the tremendous round pillars in St John's chapel which the Normans built right inside the keep.

St John's Chapel, Tower of London

Another early keep was built by Robert of Mortain at Pevensey, where he was fortunate to have the Roman stone-work of the old fort lying round, ready to be re-used. He built a rough, square keep with walls 13 ft. thick and used the Roman walls which were still standing for the curtain wall round the bailey. It had Roman round towers built into the wall at intervals.

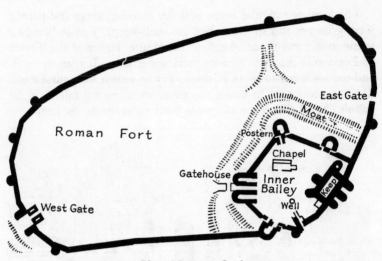

Plan of Pevensey Castle

On the Welsh border, at Chepstow, William FitzOsbern wasted little time in getting on with his castle of Striguil, as he called it. You remember that the castle was placed on a high, rocky ridge above the river Wye. William built his keep at the narrowest part of the ridge which was in the middle, so that he had two baileys, one on each side of it. The west bailey was defended on its weakest side by a deep ditch, while on the other sides there were steep precipices and a ravine. Both baileys were walled with stone and the keep stood in the strongest position between them. Its ground floor was probably used for storage and the main entrance was up a covered staircase to the first floor which was William's great hall. Along the sides of this are deep recesses, like cubicles, where William's knights probably slept. Later on the keep was altered to make it grander and more comfortable, but you can still see William FitzOsbern's stone building in the bottom part of it. Here William and his knights could lie snugly while enemies attacked their stronghold in vain.

Chepstow Castle today

When Roger de Lacy built his castle at Ludlow in Shropshire, he did not need to throw up a motte, for there was a convenient rocky mound just at the right point in a bend of the river Teme. On the landward side he dug a moat round the mound and then started to build a stone curtain all round the hill-top which was to be his inner bailey. Stone was plentiful, so he began at once on the great tower or keep which was placed in front of the gateway to guard the drawbridge over the moat. On the ground floor the entrance to the castle ran right through the keep itself. Above this was a high hall with a staircase in the thickness of the walls leading up to it. At one end of the hall was a sleeping room, and we can even see where they built their lavatories. From the hall they could step out on to the wall-walk which ran right round the top of the curtain wall. In the inner bailey there was also a well 120 ft. deep, a separate kitchen and a great oven, 12 ft. 6 in. across. Either Roger de Lacy or his successor also built the chapel of St Mary Magdalene inside the bailey. This is a round church. There are not many like this in England. Do you know one? Later castle-builders at Ludlow made a large outer bailey, with a curtain and ditch all round it, and built another great hall on the opposite side of the inner bailey. If you visit Ludlow, look out for the splendid Norman patterns carved in the chapel, especially the zigzag or *chevron* pattern.

Ludlow Castle (inner bailey)

King Henry I, one of William the Conqueror's sons, was a keen castle-builder. At Rochester he had a tremendous rectangular keep built. It was four stories high—113 ft. in all—and the walls were 12 ft. thick at the base. The main entrance was up an outside stair to the first floor. They had now discovered how to build a *portcullis* to defend the entrance. This was an especially strong door which shut down from above and had spikes at top and bottom. The door slid up and down in grooves, so that when it was raised you could walk in and out easily, but woe betide you if you got caught running in just as the portcullis, with its nasty spikes, was lowered on top of you! Rochester keep was built for comfort as well as strength. The great hall, on the second floor, had fireplaces and bigger windows than usual; there was a well from which water could be drawn on the different floors and there were lavatories in the thickness of the walls.

When Henry got back Corfe Castle into his own possession from the family of Robert of Mortain, he ordered the wooden keep to be pulled down and a strong stone one to be built, 60 ft. square and 80 ft. high. The ground floor was for stores and the great hall was on the first floor, with an outside stone staircase up to it. This was a fine piece of stone-building, much better than the rough work at Pevensey, for instance. The gate was also well defended. First there was a drawbridge over the moat and then a gatehouse flanked by two *drum-towers*. In one of these towers you can still see the slit windows, called loops, so placed that, shooting through them, you could hit anyone trying to attack the gate. By the loops you can seen the little hole in the wall to hold a pot of grease for greasing the bowstrings.

Corfe Castle today

When King Henry gave Kenilworth to his Treasurer, Geoffrey de Clinton, he built a keep 87 by 58 ft. and 80 ft. high, standing in an inner bailey. Later, other buildings and a large outer bailey were added and later still the top of the first keep blew off, but if you visit it today you can still see part of the original castle. Another splendid castle built by one of Henry's barons named William D'Albini was Castle Rising in Norfolk. The keep stands in the middle of the bailey which has a wide, deep ditch all round it. Once again, you entered the keep by an outside staircase up to the first floor. This was very carefully guarded against besiegers, for there were three doors, one at the foot, one in the middle and one at the top. If you fought your way through the bottom door on to the stairs, there was an arrow-loop from a passage above through which the defenders could snipe at you and when you had struggled up to the middle door, there was a slit over your head through which you could be attacked. So it was quite a job to capture this keep. Here are the stairs today:

William D'Albini became an important baron and when Henry I died, he married the

Staircase of Castle Rising

queen-mother and so got possession of the great Arundel Castle which Henry had given to her.

Another fine keep built at this time is Hedingham in Essex. It is four stories high and stands on a natural mound with a moat round it. On each floor there is one large hall. Once again the entrance is by an outside stair to the first floor and here the doorway into the keep is defended by a stout portcullis. Inside, a spiral staircase goes all the way up from the basement to the wall-walk on the battlements.

We have only looked at a few of the stone castles built in the time of the three Norman kings, William I and his sons William II and Henry. You must keep your eyes open to discover others as you travel about England and Wales. In this chapter I have only described the castles as we think they were between about 1066 and 1150. When you visit them today many will look different, either because they have fallen into ruin, or because since 1150 they have been altered and other walls and buildings added. When you are looking at a castle you can often discover which are the oldest parts and so trace out the pattern of the first castle. Experts do this by studying the kinds of stone used and the way the building has been done, as well as the style of the decoration.

Hedingham Castle Keep

Hedingham Castle : Great Hall

Chepstow Castle from the air

Besieging Castles

Castle-builders, of course, used all their wits to try and build a castle that could not be captured. But the very same kings and barons also had to use all their wits to find out how to capture other people's castles! Imagine yourself riding up with your army to besiege one of these castles on a motte or a rocky headland. How do you think you would tackle the job?

In the first place, I think you would send out your scouts to look for any weak points in the defences. It might be that on one side the upward slope was not so steep and so would be easier for the attack, or your scouts might find a weak place in the wooden palisade or even in a new stone wall. But remember that the defenders would also be using their wits: they would be guessing at your plans and massing their strongest forces at the weakest spots. In any case, they would hardly allow your scouts to get close up to the defences in daylight, for they would be on the watch to pick them off with well-shot arrows whenever they came within range.

There were various methods the besiegers could try. If the gate-house and palisade were of wood, they could try to set them on fire by pushing a cartful of well-greased fuel up against them and then firing it. Whilst doing this, of course, the besiegers had to keep under the shelter of the cart. Sometimes they brought a huge tree-trunk at the end of which an iron head had been fixed. This was a *battering-ram* (because the head looked like a ram) and it needed a dozen or more men to swing the head against the walls in order to make a *breach* in them. Once again, the men had to protect themselves against the defenders and so they worked under a sort of penthouse called a tortoise, which was usually covered with raw *hide* as a good protection against fire. Or the besiegers might bring scaling ladders which they tried to fix on to the walls in order to climb up. In the meantime, of course, the defenders were ready

23

Battering Ram

above them to rain down arrows or pour on their heads boiling water or red-hot metal.

The besiegers often had a tough task. This is why it was so dangerous for the king if a big baron of his refused to obey royal orders. The rebel could shut himself up in his castle and snap his fingers while the king tried to capture him. All the same, William I and his son William II (William Rufus) were good at finding ways to make rebel barons surrender. In 1088 William Rufus's uncle, Bishop Odo of Bayeux, rebelled against the king. (Although he was a bishop, he was really more of a fighting baron than anything else.) He got together with his brother, Robert of Mortain and other discontented barons; they ravaged and burned and laid waste the land, then filled their castles with knights and provisions, and defied the king. So the king gathered the biggest army he could and set out to besiege their castles. He sat down first in front of the castle of Pevensey for six weeks, but could not capture it until the garrison was starved out. He only managed this by keeping a close watch to stop food coming in by sea as well as land. Then he marched against the strong castle of Rochester. Here he tried a new siege method: he built two wooden towers or little castles to block the road to the castle and so cut off food supplies. From these towers also the besiegers could shoot over the defences into the castle bailey. Finally, the garrison surrendered, Bishop Odo and other rebel barons were banished and the country had peace for a few years. But in 1095 another big baron, Robert of Mowbray, rebelled, together with the Montgomeries. Robert shut himself up in his strong castle of Bamburgh, on a high rock, with sea and marshes all round it. The only way the king could capture it was by building a new fortress of timber on a mound as close to the castle as he could get. When he began to shoot into the castle from this, the defenders called it 'Malvoisin', which in French means 'bad neighbour'. Finally the bad neighbour was too much for them and they surrendered.

In all these cases the king finally captured the castles but there were many other times when the besieged successfully defied the besiegers. In 1094 there was a tremendous attack of the Welsh on the castle of Pembroke, held by the Montgomeries. It stood on a high cliff just at the mouth of a good harbour. Inside the castle a passage was cut down through the rock to a cave below, opening on to the sea. Here provisions were brought in secretly by boat and so, with enough food to eat, the garrison was able to beat off the attack completely. Castles, as you can see, were at this time easier to defend than attack, but the three great enemies of the defenders were Hunger, Thirst and Fire. If, however, they could keep open a way of getting in food, if they had a good, inexhaustible well inside the castle, and if they could protect the wooden stockades from fire by covering them with raw hides soaked in water, then a besieged garrison might stand a siege almost indefinitely.

Almost—but, of course, besiegers were always thinking up new ways of breaking down the defences, especially when the besiegers were powerful kings, determined to conquer rebel barons. They began to invent 'siege engines' to batter down the walls. One of the first of these was a stone-throwing machine called a *mangonel*.

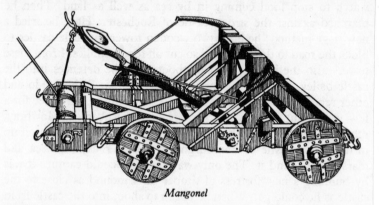

Mangonel

This could be quite small, worked by one or two men, but before long they were building a kind of tower on wheels which could be pushed up as close to the walls as possible. On it was a huge cata-pult which threw stones crashing into the walls or over them among the defenders. Then there was the *ballista*, a machine like a huge cross-bow which shot *javelins*. Wooden defences did not stand up well to this kind of battering and so, as besiegers de-veloped better machines for attack, castle-defenders had to strengthen their defences. Hence the stone walls.

Here is the story of an exciting siege in the year 1111, not in England, but in France, where King Louis VI set out to capture the castle of Le Puiset. The castle was mainly built of timber and stood on a motte. In the first place, the garrison rushed out to attack the besieging army but were driven back through the main gateway by a hailstorm of arrows. From the *ramparts* above they began to hurl down wooden planks and sharp stakes on to the king's knights. But the besiegers, throwing away their own shields as they got broken, used the wooden planks to protect themselves while they tried to fire the gateway. They dragged up carts full of dry wood smeared with fat and then there was a fierce struggle at the gate, the besiegers trying to set it alight and the defenders trying to put the fire out. Meanwhile, Theobald, one of the king's captains, was attacking from another side by climbing up the steep

Attacking a castle

side of the motte. But many of his band fell back into the ditch and others were surprised by a band of horsemen, belonging to the defenders, who were outside the castle galloping round to attack their enemies wherever they could. The king's men were almost giving up hope when a priest in the army, seizing a bit of wood to hold over his head as a shield, rushed up the motte to the wooden palisade and began tearing it down. Others followed him, chopping at the wood with axes until there was a hole big enough to jump through. Then the besiegers poured through the gap and the defenders were caught between Theobald's men on one side and this new attack on the other. They retreated to the wooden tower on the motte and, after a bit more fighting, surrendered.

Castles were useful to kings when they were guarded by faithful castellans who held them for the king, but, as you have seen, they could be very dangerous in the hands of rebels. In order to keep a tight hand on their barons English kings had two rules they tried to enforce: first, no baron was allowed to build a castle for himself without the king's permission; secondly, when a baron was the castellan of a royal castle he must surrender the keys of it when summoned to do so in the king's name. The first three Norman kings, William I, William II and Henry I, on the whole managed to make their barons obey these rules. But the next king, Stephen, had a great deal of trouble with his barons and their castles.

It arose because King Henry I died without leaving a son to succeed him, since his son had been drowned in the wreck of the White Ship. Before his death Henry made his barons promise to recognize his daughter, Matilda, as Queen of England but when he was dead another claimant, Count Stephen of Blois (Henry's nephew), arrived in England and many barons went over to his side. Perhaps it was because they did not want a woman ruling over them; perhaps because Stephen was popular with them. He was a courageous knight and an honourable man who never took a mean or unfair advantage over his enemy. Some of the barons had him crowned as king and swore oaths of homage to him. But once he was king, they soon began to rebel. Matilda was also claiming the crown and it occurred to some of the cleverer barons that they could sell their loyalty to the highest bidder, first to Stephen, then to Matilda, and then, perhaps, back to Stephen again.

Now this was where the barons' castles were so useful to them. Using his strongest castle as a centre, the rebel baron could plunder and rob far and wide in the country round, yet, if the king came against him, all he had to do was to get in provisions, bar the gates and stand the siege. So poor King Stephen had to spend a great deal of his time besieging his barons in their castles.

Very soon after his coronation messengers came hurrying to say that Baldwin de Redvers had seized the royal castle at Exeter and was lording it over the townspeople, making them give him all the provisions he needed and threatening them with fire and sword if they refused. The king, in a rage, sent 200 knights with orders to ride all night and catch Baldwin by surprise if possible. Next morning, when Baldwin's men were riding out of the castle with burning torches to throw among the citizens' houses, suddenly the king's men, with spears glittering and flags flying, galloped in

Besieging a castle

at the city gates, swooped on the rebels and chased them back into the castle. But when the king arrived with the main army, Baldwin had a very strong garrison inside the castle, all sworn to resist to death. The besiegers could see the gleaming arms of the knights encircling the castle on the walls. As they cautiously came nearer, the garrison hurled mocking shouts at them, and, when they came too near, arrows and javelins. So the siege began.

Baldwin's men were very adventurous, pouncing out of little secret *postern* gates to catch the king's men unawares and kill as many as they could before slipping back to safety. But the king, too, was very energetic. Day and night he pressed on with the siege, sometimes sending his armed men crawling up the mound to attack, sometimes putting on a whole army of slingers who rained a hail of stones on the garrison. He had men with skill in underground mining burrowing under the walls to try to bring them down. He had others building all kinds of engines, some high in the air to spy out what was going on inside the castle, some low on the ground to shake or undermine the walls. But the garrison cared nothing for all his engines.

This went on for three months and it might have done so much longer, but suddenly the two wells in the castle which always before had bubbled with an unfailing supply of water, began to dry up. When all the water was finished, the besieged drank wine and cooked with it until there was neither a drop of water nor wine left. So at last, parched by an unendurable thirst, they took counsel together and decided to send two of their leaders to the king. But he hardened his heart against them. Then Baldwin's wife, who was shut up with the garrison, came out to ask for mercy. She looked pitiful, barefooted and weeping, but still the king refused to pardon the rebels. At last all his barons came round the king to persuade him to show mercy. So he pardoned the rebels and let them leave the castle freely. As they came forth you could see how parched they were and how every man thought of nothing except rushing for water.

There was soon trouble on the Welsh border at the castle of Ludlow. Henry I had given it to one of his favourite knights, Joce de Dinan, but while King Stephen was busy elsewhere, a baron named Gervase Paganel seized it and made it a centre of rebellion against the king. After a while the king marched up to besiege Ludlow. It was a tough nut indeed! He threw up little forts from which to catapult stones into the castle, he tried to burn the gates, he tried every trick he knew, but the castle was *impregnable*. Obstinately the besiegers went on making rush attacks on the walls and obstinately the defenders threw them back. The king, who was a brave man, was often in front of the storming party. So was a young prince of Scotland. You may wonder why he was there at all. In those days, if a king wanted to make sure that another king or baron would keep a promise, he took a *hostage* from him— one of his sons, perhaps—and held him as a pledge until the promise was fulfilled. This was why King Stephen held the young son of the King of Scotland. But he treated him well and so the lad fought valiantly for him. (We shall read later about another hostage whom Stephen treated well.) In one of the attacks on Ludlow Castle the Scottish boy climbed so fast and so bravely that he got too close to one of the castle windows. Suddenly a large iron hook, called a *grappling-iron*, was thrown out of the window so cleverly that it hooked him up by the seat of his breeches and swung him up in the air. There he dangled, looking most comical, but in danger of being dragged into the castle as a prisoner. King Stephen, however, rushed to the rescue and, at the risk of being captured himself, he unhooked the boy and pulled him back to safety. In spite of all these efforts, Stephen did not succeed in capturing Ludlow before he was called away to other troubles.

While he had been busy besieging castles, Matilda had sailed across the Channel with her half-brother, Robert of Gloucester, to claim the throne for herself. They landed at Arundel, where the queen-mother, Henry I's widow, was living with her second husband, William D'Albini. These two welcomed them and declared for Matilda. All England quivered with excitement: those who favoured Matilda were jubilant: those who favoured Stephen shrank as under a fearful thunderclap. The king hurried to besiege them but found that Earl Robert had stolen away secretly to Bristol, leaving Matilda in Arundel Castle. Stephen thought about besieging her but in the end was persuaded that it was more chivalrous to let a woman go. So both Robert and Matilda got to Bristol, made a strong centre there, and began to encourage barons to rebel against Stephen.

Many terrible things were done. Barons would gather together all the knights they could, strengthen their castles, and then raid all the surrounding country, burning houses and carrying off crops and cattle to the castle. King Stephen dashed backwards and forwards trying to quell the rebels. He started to besiege Brian FitzCount in Wallingford Castle but was told it was a hopeless task and so went off towards Trowbridge Castle which was held for Miles of Gloucester, one of the chief supporters of Matilda. But this, too, he failed to capture. He kept turning from one place to another, as messengers brought news of rebellions, but sitting inside their castles the barons snapped their fingers at him.

Scaling a castle wall

There was a knight named Robert FitzHubert who was in Earl Robert's army, but he stole away stealthily with his own men and rode to Devizes, a fine and impregnable castle held for the king. Arriving outside the walls at dead of night (while the king's men slept snugly within), he stretched up to the top of the parapet scaling ladders very skilfully made of leather. Silently he and his men climbed up and, swiftly eluding the guards, seized the main garrison before they were awake. Only a few, hearing in the dead of night a shout from the storming party, took alarm and fled up into a high tower. But as they had no food, they were forced to surrender in a few days.

When Earl Robert heard how Devizes had been captured, he sent a band to claim it, but Robert FitzHubert drove them rudely away and proclaimed that he was going to hold the castle, not for Earl Robert, nor yet for King Stephen, but for himself! Very soon, however, the man who had craftily entrapped others was caught himself. He wanted Marlborough Castle which was held for the king by John the Marshal. He sent friendly messages to John asking if he would make a pact of peace with him and suggesting that he visited John in his castle. Once inside he meant to surprise the castle garrison with his own band, but John was as cunning as he and saw through his plot. So he replied in a most friendly way, gladly agreeing to his request, but as soon as Robert was inside Marlborough Castle the gates were shut and Robert was seized and thrust into a narrow dungeon. Later a grim revenge was taken, for he was hung in front of Devizes Castle.

The war between Stephen and Matilda went on, with the advantage swinging first one way and then the other. Stephen was captured at Lincoln and thrown into prison; then Earl Robert was captured at Winchester and the two important prisoners had to be exchanged. Next, Matilda took herself to Oxford where she thought she would be exceedingly safe, because of the impregnable wall and high tower of the castle and the deep waters of the River Thames washing around it. But while she rejoiced in her safety, suddenly King Stephen appeared with a large army on the other side of the river. He captured the city of Oxford very cleverly, for a spy showed him the secret of an old, deep ford across the river and he plunged gallantly in, swimming across with the first of his men and charging the enemy furiously on the other side. When the city was his, he gathered his army all round the castle where Matilda was now shut up. He ordered the guards to encircle it and to watch night and day for three months. So he hoped to starve out the garrison and capture Matilda. But when they were almost exhausted, Matilda slipped between his fingers, for she stole out of the castle with three trusty knights on a night when the snow was deep on the ground and the river thickly frozen over. Camouflaged in white, they slipped between the king's guards and over the Thames. No

33

one heard or saw them. The first thing King Stephen knew was that Matilda was safe in Wallingford, so he gave up the siege of Oxford.

In this war between Stephen and Matilda most of the barons simply played their own game. Each wanted to lord it over part of the country and all were busy building castles to make their lordship stronger. No one thought any more about getting the king's permission to do so, and thus the land was full of unlicensed castles. There was a *chronicler* (we do not know his name) who watched it all and wrote bitterly about the bad deeds of the barons on both sides. This is part of what he said:

John the Marshal, who was castellan of Marlborough, troubled the kingdom with unceasing disorder. He built castles, designed with wondrous skill, in the places that best suited him. The sons of Robert of Gloucester also built castles or stole them from their neighbours, sometimes boldly attacking their enemies in pitched battles, sometimes wasting their lands far and wide with the sword. Likewise Geoffrey de Mandeville stirred up strife in the kingdom. Where men of old had built castles in steep and precipitous places, he reconstructed them and subdued the country beneath the yoke of his power. Similarly the king's men in every county of England, sometimes with full force, sometimes in stealthy raids were putting up castles wherever they thought convenient, and everywhere the two sides turned a kingdom of joy and peace to sadness and strife.

At that time William of Dover, a man crafty and bold in warfare, relying on the Earl of Gloucester, came to the village of Cricklade in a delightful spot and with the greatest zeal built a castle which was *inaccessible* because of water and marshes on every side, and with a large following of knights and archers he made *forays* in every direction, restless and merciless. Sometimes laying ambushes by night, sometimes making fierce and furious raids on his enemies' castles, he harassed the country far and wide.

You can tell that the chronicler hated to see these pleasant villages so disturbed. It was always the country farmers and peasants who suffered most in these cruel raids.

Stephen went on energetically dashing about from one siege to another, and gradually he became more successful in capturing castles. The chronicler tells us about two successful sieges. He arrived at Winchcombe where Roger, Earl of Hereford, had built a castle on a high mound with very steep sides. It looked impregnable, but Stephen heard that the garrison was small, so he gave orders that the most vigorous men should storm up the steep slope as fast as possible. Some were to advance upright, shooting clouds of arrows in front of them, others were to crawl up the mound, and everyone else was ordered to rush rapidly round the castle, throwing anything that was handy. The king and his men strove so fiercely that the defenders gave in and surrendered the castle.

For the siege of another castle at Faringdon, Stephen fetched up siege engines most skilfully made and posted a dense ring of archers all round. The besieged were in a bad position. On the one hand, stones launched from the engines were battering them to bits; on the other hand, a most fearful hail of arrows flew around before their eyes. Sometimes javelins were hurled in, sometimes sturdy warriors, gallantly climbing the steep rampart, fought them at the palisade. The besieged fought back manfully, but at last the commander secretly sent to the king and agreed to surrender the castle.

So one by one the castles fell and King Stephen won back his kingdom. Matilda gave up the fight, but Stephen was forced to agree that Matilda's son, Henry, should succeed him as king. So, in the year 1154, the young Henry became King Henry II.

Life in a Twelfth-century Castle

King Henry II meant to have no nonsense about unlicensed castles. He ordered many of the temporary castles which barons had run up quickly during Stephen's reign to be pulled down. And he saw that his orders were obeyed. So today you can see in some parts of England grass mounds which are destroyed castles. But he still needed very strong castles of his own and he still wished his most faithful and trusted barons to have good strongholds. So, after 1154, that is, in the second half of the twelfth century, we find a great deal of castle repairing and strengthening going on. By this time the earth mottes which the Normans had thrown up had been standing for nearly a hundred years. The earth had settled down and the mottes would now stand the weight of heavy stone building. So a number of great stone keeps were built at this time. Henry's castles cost him quite a lot. We know some of the amounts he paid because he made his Treasurer keep careful accounts on

Dover Castle

long rolls of parchment, called Pipe Rolls because they looked like drainpipes when rolled up. On these Pipe Rolls the Treasurer's clerks wrote down the sums spent on castles (as well as many other things).

Henry paid most attention to castles set at important points to mount guard against possible enemies. High on the cliff above Dover was the castle which watched against French invaders. Henry II spent £5,000 on it. He built a strong inner bailey, with a high curtain and square, projecting towers. The two gates were guarded by extra fortifications.

In the bailey he built a square keep which was one of the strongest and most elaborate in the country. It is 83 ft. high, with square turrets rising another 12 ft. The walls are from 17 to 21 ft. thick. The entrance was by a long outside flight of stairs which went round one corner up to the first floor and then up again to the second floor. Look at this plan of the first floor:

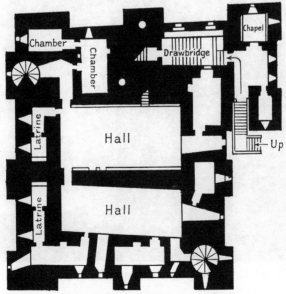

Dover Castle. Plan of Keep (first floor)

Dover Castle: stairway in the Keep

38

The keep has two chapels and four halls. The entrance is guarded by a drawbridge. Can you see the postern to one side of it? From this the defenders could pounce on enemies trying to force their way up the stair. The two spiral staircases at opposite corners led right down to the basement and up to the battlements. The well is 350 ft. deep. All the various halls and chambers were needed because there was generally a large garrison living in Dover Castle. They were well provided with lavatories. Can you find them?

Another great keep built by Henry II, though much smaller than Dover, was at Newcastle, guarding the river Tyne. You should be able to say who the enemy was for whom the garrison watched. Henry spent £911 10s. 9d. on this castle. Once again it was very strongly fortified but also built to live in. It had separate chambers in the thickness of the wall, fireplaces, proper lavatories and even pipes carrying water from the deep well to various parts of the keep.

Henry had other strong keeps built, like great watch-dogs guarding the northern border and sea-coast at Scarborough, Bamburgh, Middleham, Norham, Appleby and Carlisle. Again, there was need to keep strong castles on the border between England and Wales. I think you will know why. So we find on the Pipe Rolls money being spent strengthening the castles at Chester, Shrewsbury, Clun, Bridgenorth, Hereford, Goodrich and Gloucester.

All these were rectangular keeps. It was convenient to make them square or oblong because you could fit the halls and chambers neatly inside. But a keep with sharp corners had one very great disadvantage: an enemy who started mining under the walls could only be attacked from one side, since the corner would shelter him from any other attack. So castle-builders began to experiment with different-shaped castles which

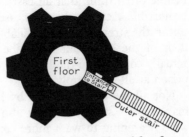

Conisbrough Keep. Plan of first floor

39

Conisbrough Keep as it probably looked

had less sharp corners. Some were many-sided or *polygonal* and some were circular. On the previous page is the plan of the first floor of a polygonal castle.

Now look at the picture of Conisbrough Castle from the outside and try in imagination to fit the plan inside it.

Orford Castle in Suffolk was another polygonal keep built by Henry II against invasion on the east coast. It has 21 sides on the outside, including three projecting turrets, but inside it is circular. One way to arrive at a circular keep was to build up a round tower inside an old shell-keep. This is what Henry II did at Windsor. You remember that at Berkeley, William FitzOsbern had built a wooden castle on a motte? This castle fell into Henry's hands at the death of Stephen and he made the new owner, Robert Fitzharding, build a strong circular keep which encased some of the old motte in its base.

I am sure you will be asking where the castle dungeons were. People often think that all castles have special dungeons built to be horrible. Actually, in many cases, this was not so. Prisoners were put in the strongest place available which was often the basement floor of the keep, but might be anywhere. The word dungeon actually comes from the French word donjon which does not mean prison at all but simply keep.

Not all the building done by Henry II and his barons was to make castles stronger. They also had to be lived in and people were beginning to want more comfort in their castles. The king himself did not live in one or two palaces, but travelled about continually in England and in his French lands, staying in his castles and hunting-lodges. He needed a great hall in which to hold court and give feasts, and by this time halls might have fireplaces so that men could be well warmed while they made merry. Then Henry would need a King's Chamber for himself and his splendid Queen Eleanor must have a Queen's Bower. There would probably be fireplaces in these as well. Again, there must be separate rooms for the royal family, important members of the royal household and royal guests. Of course there must be good kitchens near the hall. People were getting more particular in their habits, too: they liked fresh water to drink and to wash in and they liked decent lavatories or latrines. These were often called *garderobes* and you will find them marked on the plans of some castles. Of course the great barons wanted to be as up to date as the king in their castles. When the keep itself was not suitable for the living quarters, they often built a separate hall with kitchens at one end and various chambers at the other end, and perhaps a chapel as well. They did

Oakham Castle Hall

this at Oakham Castle. One of Henry II's great bishops, Hugh Pudsey, built a splendid hall along the curtain wall of the inner

Doorway to great hall, Durham Castle

bailey at Durham. It had three stories and on the first floor you entered the great hall through the magnificent doorway opposite. Sometimes the rooms for living in were just built of wood and so have now completely disappeared. But still, in many castles, the people living there had to make themselves as comfortable as they could in the great rectangular or circular keeps. This meant living inside thick stone walls and running up and down a great many winding staircases. In spite of their 'modern conveniences' I think we should have found it very cold and draughty. Look at the plans and pictures in this chapter and imagine what it would be like to live in these places.

If you had been a boy or girl growing up in a twelfth-century castle, even in peacetime I think you would have found plenty going on round about you. In the first place, there would be the normal castle garrison. Many of the knights owning lands round-about had the duty of doing castle-guard, for the king in the case of a royal castle, or for the baron who was lord of the castle. This meant that they had to send so many men in turn to garrison the castle for one or two months at a time. The size of the garrison varied: at Richmond in Yorkshire it was only 26 men in winter, but went up to 42 in summertime when the Scottish raiders were likely to appear; at Dover it was 23 at a time and at Hastings only 12. These men probably slept and ate their meals in the great hall and you would see them clattering up and down the stairway which led to the *battlements*, where they kept watch by turn. Imagine yourself, perhaps, climbing up to that windy walk which runs all round the top of the keep and marching round with the guard who watch the countryside or the river to spy out every-one approaching the castle. Or you may descend right down to ground level and go to see what the castle servants are doing at their various jobs in the inner or outer bailey.

Grinding a sword

43

You may find the grooms in the stables currying the horses, the blacksmith at his forge beating out a sword or sharpening one, and the carpenter making a bench for the hall or a cradle for a new baby. The stonemason is generally occupied looking for and repairing weak places in the walls; the arrow-maker or *fletcher* will be whittling away busily, piling up sheaves of arrows for the great long-bows which he looks after so carefully. The lord's huntsmen —if they are not scouring the countryside to see where the beasts lie—will be looking to their hounds, and the *falconers* feeding the hooded hawks on their perches (carefully keeping their fingers away from those cruel beaks). On a special grass plot the washerwoman is spreading linen to dry and one of the cooks is picking herbs for flavouring in the little herb-garden. As it is peacetime, the gates lie open and the drawbridge over the moat is down. Trundling up the steep slopes and rumbling over the bridge come the country carts full of things the castle folk need—meat, flour, barley, firewood, hay and so on. For the peasants in the surrounding villages are mostly tenants of the lord and must work in the lord's fields and harvest his crops. Some may be bringing live sheep or hens or geese to be kept till needed.

If you now go back into the keep, everyone seems equally busy. The cooks are scurrying backwards and forwards in the kitchen, stirring the huge cauldron of stew, mixing sauces, pulling loaves out of the oven and shouting at the boy who turns the spit on which great joints of meat are roasting. In the great hall servants are scrubbing the *pewter tankards* with sand and laying fresh rushes on the floor. In the little chapel the family chaplain has finished saying Mass and is carefully putting his vestments in their chest. The lady of the castle is in her bower with the sewing women. They must work hard, for they spin and weave much cloth as well as sewing for the castle people. If there is time to spare, the lady probably likes to get away from the dull jobs and embroider a piece of tapestry in brilliant colours to hang behind her chair, perhaps, in the great hall. In his own chamber the lord of the castle sits doing business with his *steward*. They must go over accounts together, discuss the lord's tenants and their lands and perhaps talk about the castle defences. Beside this, the steward may be getting ready to ride off to one of the lord's manors, where he will hold a court for the lord and settle all the disputes. The lord really has to govern a great many tenants and their affairs. If this castle is the centre or head of his *honour*, that is, of all his lands, he will often hold an important court in the castle itself for all his tenants.

That was only an imaginary picture of what you might have found going on, but it brings in most of the important things that had to be attended to if you lived in a castle. Garrison, armour and weapons, food-supplies, strong walls—these were the most vital things the lord of a castle had to think about. But there were other things in life as well: governing your people well, teaching your sons to be good knights, hunting and sporting, feasting and making music, worshipping God and making yourself ready for the sudden death which might come at any moment. Every good lord tried to leave to his children more lands than he had inherited and he would share them out carefully among his family in his last will and testament.

In the keep was the *armoury*, with the lord's *armourer* in charge of this most important part of the establishment. If you went to watch a knight arming there, you would see that first he put on a *hauberk*, that is, a shirt made of tiny linked rings of iron, called ring-mail or chain-mail. Some knights wore a padded leather tunic, called a *gambeson*, under this shirt of mail. Then probably your knight would protect his legs with coverings of ring-mail, called *chausses*. Then he would

Figure of knight in armour from a tomb

45

gird on his sword-belt and sword. Last of all he would put on his helmet. In the armoury there were many of these hanging up. Some were old-fashioned ones—the sort men wore at the Battle of Hastings about a hundred years before. These were *conical* in shape and had no covering for the face except a nosepiece. But the newest fashion in helmets was a large, flat-topped one which covered the whole head. I expect all the younger knights in the garrison wanted to be up to date in their helmets. These new ones protected your face, but they had two disadvantages—they were heavy to wear and while you wore one nobody could see who you were. So, in battle and tournament, knights were just beginning to wear badges on their shields and on top of their helmets to distinguish themselves. A little later these became the family badges we call *coats of arms*, but in the twelfth century they were just personal badges chosen by each knight. Some knights put a sleeveless linen tunic, called a *surcoat*, over their hauberks and they often had their own badge embroidered on this coat. That is why we speak of a coat of arms.

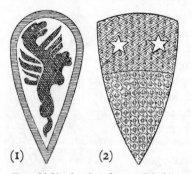

(1)   (2)

Two shields showing change of fashion

There were fashions in shields as well as helmets. You could tell if a knight was using his father's shield because it would be shaped like a long kite (1), while the newer ones were like (2).

Now, with sword, helmet and shield complete, your knight only needs to pick a good stout *lance* from the armoury and he

Getting out of a hauberk

46

will be ready. But, though this armour is not as heavy as it will be two centuries later, it is heavy enough, and if your knight has only been dressing-up to show you he will be anxious to get his helmet and hauberk off. It was quite difficult to get out of this heavy chain-mail, as the picture on the opposite page shows.

You must try to imagine what it would be like to rush up a scaling-ladder with all that on.

It was the armourer's duty to inspect all the armour and weapons regularly and give the blacksmith his orders. Weak links in chain-mail must be repaired at once, lest a sword or lance thrust, or even an arrow might pierce through. Dents must be hammered out of helmets, swords kept sharp and polished, lances inspected closely, for if the *shaft* was weak it might splinter to bits at the first thrust. Besides the equipment for the knights, the arms of the archers and ordinary foot-soldiers had to be attended to. Great long-bows made of yew were always ready, unstrung until needed because this kept the spring in the wood, but with the bowstrings always well greased. Sheaves of arrows were ready, with battle-axes, spears and long knives as well. For armour these men usually had padded leather tunics and helmets.

Of course when you were assaulting or defending a castle, fighting had mainly to be done on foot and you needed to be a strong knight to pound up the steep slope of a motte carrying all that weight of armour. But the real way a knight liked to fight was on horse-back, with the horse carrying the weight! It had to be a heavy war-horse, called a *charger*, and the lord of a castle usually had many of these in his stables, besides less powerful baggage-horses, hunting-horses, small horses called *palfreys* for the ladies, and cart-horses. It took a lot of training to ride your horse squarely at your enemy, strike home with your lance, unhorse him and not fall off yourself! *Tournaments*, which were really mock-battles, gave knights a chance to practise for real battles, as well as competing for prizes. Of course, if you did not want to look ridiculous, you had to train hard for the tournaments themselves. So, any fine day, you would probably have seen the young knights and squires practising in the outer bailey of the castle. They had to learn to ride their horses at the gallop with the lance held at full tilt, ready to strike home at its target. As they struck, they had to check sharply and wheel the horse round quickly to avoid the opponent's blow. In order to practise this, knights would set up a *quintain* and ride full tilt at it. This was a stand with two revolving arms on which hung a shield and a sand-bag. The game was to ride up at the gallop, strike the shield with your lance, and then

Riding at the Quintain

wheel out of the way before the sand-bag swung round and hit you. There was sword-practice also, for the second round of a tournament was often fought on foot with swords. You will understand now why the practising place was often called a *tilting-yard*. Squires and knights had to spend much time practising here before they could hope to be successful at a tournament. There were also targets for archery, called *butts*, where the archers practised shooting.

All this was good sport as well as training for warfare. The castle garrison was not likely to be bored even in peacetime, for there was plenty of sport and amusement. When the countryside was peaceful, the lord, with his men, would ride out merrily across the drawbridge when the first sunbeams were beginning to sparkle on the trees to go hawking. The powerful hawks and *falcons* would be perched, bound and hooded, on their wrists, apparently fast asleep. Suddenly, with a whirr of wings, the party would rouse up the birds they were after—quails, cranes, wild geese, etc. Then quickly one of the hawkers would slip off the hood and leather strap binding the hawk and instantly he would come to life, mounting up and up into the blue sky above his *quarry* and then swooping suddenly and terribly to strike the poor bird with his cruel beak and bring him down. Each sportsman had his own hawk and they would play one against the other to see which was the best.

They might take the dogs to go hunting the hare or the fox, or in wintertime there might be an exciting boar-hunt. This could be dangerous, for wild *boars* had strong, sharp tusks and might charge at the huntsmen when angry. Above all, they liked to hunt the shy wild deer through the deep forest, but no lord could hunt just where and what he pleased, for there were large stretches of

country called royal forests where no one could hunt unless the king gave him permission. King Henry II loved hunting, especially the red deer, and if you had been a huntsman in a royal castle, you would have been busy all the time, tracking down the deer, keeping the horses and hounds in good shape, preparing for the hunt. Then, late one night perhaps, the king would come riding in from some distant castle. He would throw himself down to sleep, but next morning you would have to be ready to be up and off by dawn to the green wood with him, and woebetide you if you did not find the deer where you said they were! King Henry could get very angry! He would hunt furiously, come back to the castle, hold a solemn council on important government business, feast long, sleep a little, and be up again at sunrise to ride to the next place where he would stay. Henry II was a restless, energetic king.

There were plenty of indoor games for stormy winter days. Chess, backgammon and dice were popular. Grown-ups enjoyed what we should call children's games, and the great hall was a fine place for a jolly game of blindman's-buff or battledore and shuttlecock. Round dances and long dances went merrily to the sound of pipe and drum or a very early kind of fiddle. Of course people got rowdy sometimes and even quarrelsome. There is a story about two brothers playing dice in the *solar* above the great hall; they made a terrific noise and tried to pour water on their third brother down below. He rushed into the hall with his sword drawn and only their father was able to stop the fight, but this quarrel started a feud which went on for years.

Nobody ate much breakfast, for they all got busy as soon as the sun rose; a hunk of bread and a drink of ale was probably enough as you went off to your work or your sport. You might sit down to a large dinner in the afternoon or later in the evening but, whenever it came, everyone was ready for it. Work was done, so now you could enjoy yourself. Dinner was the thing, and most people could eat a lot more at once than we can. It was all done with great ceremony. The torches round the walls of the great hall would be flaring in their *sconces*, the fires would blaze and the lord would be seated in his great chair at the high table, with his lady, their children and his chief knights and guests. Everyone else had his proper place at the long wooden tables which stretched down the length of the hall. From the doors at the far end would come the procession of serving-men with great steaming dishes and, if it were a great feast, the procession would be led by trumpeters. The first dishes would be carried up to the high table and there the pages and squires would carve the meat and serve the diners on bended knee. They would pour wine into the silver drinking goblets and bring basins of water and napkins to wash fingers which were used instead of forks. The rest of the company did not eat so elegantly—they picked pieces from the dishes with their fingers and drank from pewter tankards. The meal went on a long time, as you can guess from this sample menu:

1. Boar's head with tusks in its snout, garnished with flowers.

2. Venison, cranes, peacocks, swans, kids, pigs, hens.
3. Spiced and seasoned meats with red and white wine in great plenty.
4. Pheasants, woodcock, partridges, larks and plovers, well-roasted, with brawn and other things.
5. White powder (blancmange) and large sweetmeats.

It was exciting to be a boy living in a great castle. Many barons liked to send their sons to be educated in the household of some other lord who would promise to train them as good knights. First, you would serve as a page. This part of your education had a lot to do with good manners. Here are some instructions from a book which told 'babies', that is, small pages, how to behave:

> Fair Babies, when you enter your lord's place say 'God speed' and salute all there. Hold up your head and kneel on one knee to your lord. If any speak to you, look straight at them and listen well. Answer sensibly and shortly. Stand till you are told to sit down, keep your hands and feet quiet and don't scratch yourself. Bow to your lord when you answer him. Be always ready to serve at the proper times, to bring drink, hold lights or anything else. When your lord is ready for dinner, pour out water and hold the towel till he has finished. Stand by your lord till he tells you to sit. Cut your bread, don't break it. Don't lean on the table or dirty the cloth, or hang your head over your dish or eat with a full mouth. Don't dip your meat in the salt-cellar or put your knife in your mouth or make a noise eating. When the meal is over, clean your knives and put them in their places, rise without laughing and joking and go to your lord's table and stand there till grace is said.

I am sure the pages had lots of fun with each other but their education was strict. Is it more strict than yours?

In your teens you became a squire and began the warlike part of your education. You would probably become the squire of one particular lord. You learnt to keep his armour well and dress him in it correctly. You saw to his horses and when he went to a tournament or on a war expedition, you accompanied him. You were not allowed to fight yourself but one of your special duties was to lead and guard your lord's baggage-horses. In a tournament your part was rather like that of a second in a boxing match: you would look after your knight when he came out of the fray and take bits of battered armour to be repaired for next day. Your polite education went on at the same time: you learnt to carve neatly at dinner, to dance elegantly and to sing and perhaps play a musical instrument. All the time you would be watching and learning about warfare. You would learn how to put on armour, to balance your lance on horse-back and use your sword. You would ride at the quintain until you had got the trick quite perfect. But so long as you were a squire, you had to keep in the background: you could not compete in a tournament and if you tried to get in the front battle-line you would be ordered back severely.

So every squire looked forward eagerly to the day when his education would be over and he would be knighted. This might happen suddenly on a battlefield, but often it was a solemn ceremony planned beforehand. The young man would take a bath, put on fresh clothes and a beautiful new cloak, and kneel before the one who was to knight him. This lord would dub him a knight by striking him on the shoulder with his sword and then gird on his sword-belt and sword. The great thing was to be knighted by a great prince or lord whom you admired very much.

These barons and knights did not mind about hard knocks and bloodshed. Indeed, they seemed to revel in fighting. Most of the fighting was done in summertime, so they looked forward eagerly to the springtime, not so much because it brought bright flowers and bird-songs as because they could begin to furbish up their armour and get ready for battle. One of the great troubadours sang a spring-song which went like this:

> Spring is the time when knights go out to war, when the meadows are white with *pavilions*, when shepherds and their flocks scurry away from the advance-guards of armies, when the earth trembles beneath the hooves of chargers, when castles are *beleaguered* and walls and towers crumble down in ruin.

But they thought about other things besides fighting. We have not so far talked much about the ladies in the castle. The lord's wife often had girls for whose education she was responsible, just as the lord was for the boys'. Then there were her own daughters and her waiting-ladies. So there were often a number of attractive girls in the castle and of course knights and squires fell in love. Knights would often have their own special ladies and wear their favours in tournaments. They thought of the prizes won as honours to their ladies and, if they were able, would write love-songs to them. If he could not do it himself, a knight would pay a *troubadour* to write and sing songs to his lady. Here is one of these little love-songs translated into English:

'When I see the lark raise its wings in joy against the sun's rays and then, oblivious, let itself fall, because of the sweetness which fills its heart, then such great envy fills me of those whom I see happy, that I wonder my heart does not melt with desire.

'Alas! I thought I knew so much about love, and I know so little! For I cannot help loving her from whom I will gain nothing. She has taken my heart, and taken myself, and her own self and all the world, and when she took herself from me, she left me only desire and a yearning heart.'

(by Bernart de Ventadorn)

A knight did not often marry his lady-love. Marriage was thought of rather as a business matter: you must marry a girl with lands for her *dowry*, or, better still, a rich heiress whose possessions would make you more powerful. Often these marriages were quite happy ones, but, all the same, you enjoyed your romantic little dream of a lady-love.

Here is a little story about a love-sick squire:

Fair and fairer still than I can say was Blonde, the Earl of Oxford's daughter. She sat at dinner and was served by Jehan the squire, fair and free of body, who pained himself much to earn all men's grace by his *courteous* service. He waited not on his lady alone, but up and down throughout the hall, knight and lady, squire and page, groom and messenger, all he served according to their desire and thus from all he earned goodwill.

After dinner they washed their hands and went to play, each as he would, up in the forest or down by the river or in some other sort of

53

pastime. Jehan would go with whom he would and on his return oftentimes would he go to play in the Countess's bower. Well he knew all chamber games—chess and backgammon and dice—wherewith he *diverted* the lady Blonde.

One day, as Blonde sat at table, it was for Jehan to carve before her. By chance he cast his eyes on her; yet he had seen her daily these 18 weeks past. From this look such thoughts came into his head that on his carving he thought no more. Blonde, who marked his thoughts astray, took upon her to rebuke him therefore, and bade him think on his carving without delay. Seeing then that Jehan heard her not for the moment, then spake she again: 'Carve, Jehan! Are you sleeping or dreaming here? I pray you, give me now to eat; of your courtesy, dream no more.' At this word Jehan heard her voice; therewith he started as one who is shaken suddenly from his sleep. He seized the knife as a man in a dream and thought to carve well and fair, but so *distraught* was he that he cut deep into two fingers; forth sprang the blood as he rose from table and sad was Blonde at that sight. Jehan prayed another squire to carve before his lady and went forthwith to his own chamber.

In the dark winter evenings knights and ladies liked to listen to troubadour songs about love and war. Some of these were long story-poems called *ballads*, about great deeds in battle or the adventures of knights and ladies. The latest fashion in the time of Henry II were stories about King Arthur and his knights. Of course the real Arthur had lived hundreds of years before this, but people in the twelfth century loved stories about him and imagined Arthur and his knights dressed in the same armour and riding to the same kind of tournaments as they did themselves.

Fighting was natural to these knights and they could hardly stop themselves doing it, but they knew that warfare could be brutal so they wanted to have a good excuse for it—a good cause to fight for. One good reason was loyalty. Knights took *oaths of fealty*, or faithfulness, to their lords and if the lord summoned his vassal to fight, the knight's duty was to support him through thick and thin, whatever the cause of the war might be. Men also believed that it was right to fight in defence of the old and the weak, and especially ladies. Many of the Arthur stories are about knights rescuing ladies. I am afraid, however, that these knights did not think much about protecting poor, defenceless peasants. Thirdly, every good knight wished to fight for God. This usually meant fighting the heathen Saracens who were conquering Palestine and swarming along the Mediterranean even as far as Spain. When they captured Christians they made them slaves to row in their galleys or took them far off into pagan lands. It was a great heroic adventure for a knight to take the vow of a Crusader and go off to fight in far and strange places. He might spend years as a slave, he might never return, but he believed he would be using his strength and skill to fight for God.

Much of the time, however, barons and knights were occupied in much less noble warfare nearer home. There might be long peacetimes, but often your enemies were on the watch to make trouble when they could. Here is the story of some of the troubles at Ludlow Castle in the time of Henry II. You remember that the Lord of Ludlow, Joce de Dinan, had been turned out of it in the reign of Stephen. Henry II gave it back to him and Joce perhaps hoped for a quiet life in it. But at least he prepared for trouble by pushing on with strengthening the walls and turning the gatehouse into a strong keep. Trouble soon came to him, for his neighbour, Hugh de Mortimer, was his enemy, ready to pounce at any moment. Matters grew so bad that Joce was almost a prisoner in his own castle, hardly daring even to go out hunting. One day, however, Joce discovered that Hugh was going to ride out alone, instead of with his usual armed band. So he laid an ambush, captured him and took him back in triumph to Ludlow, where he was kept a prisoner in a high round tower until he paid a ransom of 3,000 marks. The tower is still called Mortimer's tower.

But Joce had another enemy—Hugh de Lacy—who claimed some of his lands. We know many stories about this feud because they are told in a long story-poem called *The Romance of the Fitz-Warines*. There was a boy named Fulk FitzWarine who was sent at the age of seven to be educated in Joce de Dinan's household. He must have found it a very exciting life. When he was about 18 the feud between Joce and Hugh de Lacy was at its fiercest. Looking out one morning from the highest tower Joce saw the meadows

Ludlow Castle: Mortimer's Tower

gleaming with spears as de Lacy's army rode towards the castle. Hastily Joce gathered together his men, about 500 of them, and charged out to the attack so fiercely that de Lacy's men turned tail in flight. Joce saw de Lacy riding away alone and, galloping after him, was just about to take him prisoner when three of de Lacy's men dashed up and attacked Joce. Inside the castle Joce's wife and her two daughters, Sybil and Hawyse, had been anxiously watching the fight. When they saw Joce set on by three men they shrieked out so loudly that young Fulk FitzWarine (who had, of course, not been in the fight) came rushing to find out what distressed them so much. The Lady Hawyse taunted him with remaining safe inside the castle while her father was in danger of his life and, stung by her scorn, the young Fulk rushed out of the castle into the fray. So successful was his help that he and Joce killed two of the enemy and brought back de Lacy and one knight named Arnold de Lys as prisoners.

Among the ladies in the castle was a beautiful girl named Marion de la Bruere who fell in love with the prisoner Arnold. He persuaded her to help the two of them to escape. So one dark night they made a rope from pieces of linen and slid down the curtain wall from a window. De Lacy went on attacking Joce whenever he could and made himself such a nuisance all through the district that finally some neighbouring barons insisted on their making up the quarrel in order to get a little peace. By this time the Lady Hawyse, although she had once been so scornful of him, was betrothed to Fulk FitzWarine. There was a splendid wedding at Ludlow, with much feasting and rejoicing, and at the end of it Joce and all his household rode away to pay a visit in Berkshire, leaving only 30 knights and 70 soldiers behind.

They left someone else behind, however. Marion de la Bruere had pretended to be too ill to go but really she was planning to see her lover Arnold again. She sent him a message saying that Joce had only left a small garrison and he at once told de Lacy. Together they planned to surprise the castle. On a moonless night Arnold, with a hundred men, came creeping up under the castle wall. There Marion was waiting at a window to drop down a cord. To this Arnold attached a leather ladder which she drew up. When the garrison were sleeping Arnold and his men slipped up the ladder, killed the guard and captured the castle. In the morning Marion realized how treacherous she had been and, suddenly seized with despair, she snatched her lover's sword, killed him as he slept and flung herself to death from a window.

But de Lacy still had Ludlow Castle and when Joce, who was enjoying himself at Lambourn, heard the news he was very angry. Joce and his son-in-law, Fulk, raised a large army and besieged Ludlow furiously. The siege went on a long time, for both sides were very determined. Once Joce nearly got the castle. He succeeded in burning down part of the outer gateway with a fire of bacon grease and got inside the outer bailey. But de Lacy got Welsh reinforcements who turned the tables on Joce. Finally he was captured and imprisoned in his own castle.

The only thing to be done was to appeal to the king. Fulk and his wife Hawyse fled to Henry II's court where their complaints were heard. Hawyse was made a lady-in-waiting to Queen Eleanor and Henry ordered de Lacy to release Joce. He did so because he feared the king's armies. So Joce came to court and soon afterwards his grandson, another Fulk, was born. Poor Joce never got back his castle of Ludlow. He died soon after and left it to his son-in-law, Fulk FitzWarine, but although Fulk was a brave soldier he never managed to get hold of Ludlow again. Nor did the next Fulk, Joce's grandson. He was outlawed by King John and had many exciting adventures like Robin Hood.

Not all castles, of course, had such troubled times as Ludlow. Remember, this was in the Welsh border country where there were always more raids and skirmishes than elsewhere. The Welsh themselves were generally ready to come in and help in any fighting and the king with his army was usually far away. King Henry, however, was determined to stop this sort of thing as much as he could. He was quite successful in making his barons keep the peace and was helped in this work by his most loyal barons. In the next chapter you will read the story of one of the most faithful knights in the twelfth century.

A Twelfth-century Knight:
William the Marshal

If you were a poor but ambitious knight in the twelfth century, the way to get on in the world was to train yourself to be a good soldier and so attract the eye of the king. There was an unknown knight named Gilbert who only owned a few lands in Wiltshire, but he fought stoutly for Henry I who made him Marshal of his court as a reward. His job was to be one of the king's chief captains when he went to war and in peacetime to arrange the big state ceremonies when the king solemnly wore his crown. Gilbert's son, John Fitz-Gilbert, was a tough man too, and managed to hang on to the office of Marshal, though he had to fight for it. He was called John the Marshal, or sometimes just John Marshal. When Stephen became king, John took his side at first. He captured two important Wiltshire castles, Marlborough and Ludgershall, and pretended to hold them for King Stephen. Do you remember how Robert Fitz-Hulbert invited John Marshal to join him in capturing and keeping castles for themselves? And do you remember how John tricked him? John was playing his own game and was determined to make as much as he could out of the war. So he always tried to stay on the winning side. When Stephen was captured he went over to Matilda's side and he had some exciting adventures fighting for her. Once he was escorting her to his castle of Ludgershall when his little band was attacked by a much larger force. Sending Matilda galloping on to safety with one of his faithful retainers, he held the enemy back, fighting on until he and his men were beaten. With one follower he took refuge in Wherwell Abbey Church. When his opponents set fire to it, they climbed the tower. The heat grew so intense that it melted the lead roof and a drop of molten lead blinded John in one eye. But he refused to surrender and at last the enemy went away, thinking they must have been burnt. But not a bit of it! John and his man came out and galloped off to Ludgershall.

John remained faithful to Matilda's party for some time. He was very good at tricking his enemies. One day an enemy leader sent a message to him at Ludgershall: 'If you will wait one day for us, we will come and fight you.' John Marshal sent back a message saying that of course he would not wait for them. So the enemy thought John was running away and when they set out next day for Ludgershall, they rode easily and did not even put their helmets on. But John had come to meet them instead and suddenly he pounced on them from an ambush in the woods. Although a bigger army, all the men took fright and ran away. John managed to capture Newbury Castle, so that now he held three castles. Between these he was able to lord it all through Wiltshire and Berkshire. Do you remember reading on page 34 what the chronicler thought about his bad deeds?

John had several sons. William was his fourth and while all these exciting fights were going on, he was a very little boy, probably living in the castle at Marlborough. One day, when he was five or six years old, he had a terrible adventure. King Stephen's army appeared at Newbury and encircled the castle. John knew there were very few men with very little food inside and that they could not stand a long siege. He asked for a *truce*. This meant that he had to promise not to put reinforcements inside the castle while the truce lasted, and, as a pledge that he would keep his promise, he gave Stephen his son William as a hostage. But the cruel John had no intention of keeping his promise: he had more sons and one did not matter so him as much as his castle. So he rushed men and food into Newbury Castle in order that it could stand a siege. He told the King's messengers that they could hang William if they liked, for he had the anvils and hammers with which to forge better sons.

So there was poor little William in the enemy camp, in the hands of a king who was very angry because his father had broken his promise and tricked him. According to the rules of warfare Stephen had the right to kill his hostage in revenge and this he resolved to do. William understood nothing of what was going on and had no idea that he was about to be killed, but he remembered to the end of his days what happened next. When he was an old and famous man he told his son the story and a troubadour put it into a long poem. This poem is in French, but, put into English, this is the story of William's adventure:

As the boy was being led along, not dreaming he was going to his death, he saw the Earl of Arundel holding a very fine hunting-spear, and he said innocently: 'Sire, give me that spear!' When the King heard this childish remark, he would not allow him to be hanged that day, no, not for all the gold of France, but he took the boy in his arms and said: 'You are reprieved from this agonizing death; of a truth, you shall not die today.' They returned to the army and found the mangonel being got ready for hurling stones into the castle. Then some of the king's wicked counsellors advised the king to take the boy straightway, place him in the sling of the mangonel and have him flung at the castle to strike terror into the defenders. The boy, little suspecting, was led up to the mangonel; he saw the sling and exclaimed: 'Goodness! What a big seesaw! Do let me have a go at it!', and he leant up against the sling. The King said: 'Let be! Let be! It would be wicked indeed to let him die in such torments. His childish sayings are so pretty. Collect stones for the siege engines, as heavy as you can manage.'

Some then worked the mangonel, while others made screens of hurdles to cover themselves as they attacked the gate. One of the ruffians dragged William out in front of the castle and called out to the defenders: 'Here is the son of your lord and we are going to place him on top of the hurdles when we attack.' But they replied from the castle: 'Then he is doomed, for we shall squash him as flat as a pancake!' A great millstone was then hung out from the battlements, ready to drop on the hurdle-screens when they attacked. William thereupon enquired what new kind of game they were hanging out of the window. The king laughed heartily and said: 'William, that game would not be good for you! Playthings such as that shall never be given to you. You shall never die by my command!'

So King Stephen saved William, but he kept the boy as a hostage in his camp for many weeks. William was quite at home there; he played games with the soldiers and sometimes he even asked the king to play with him. Do you ever play the game of conkers?

There is another game like it which you play with plantains. These have long stems and heads and each player tries to strike off the head of the other player's plantain or 'knight'. This is the story of how William played 'knights' with King Stephen:

The king was resting one day during the siege. He was sitting in his tent which was strewn with grass and flowers of many colours. William saw the flowers and went up and down looking at them. Eagerly and happily he set about picking up the 'knights'. When he had gathered enough in his fist, he said to the king: 'Fair and dear lord, would you like a game of "knights"?' 'Yes, indeed, fair, sweet friend,' replied the other. 'Which of us shall strike first?' said William. 'You,' said the king, 'my fair and honoured friend.' So William took one of his knights and the king held out one of his towards it, and the result of this encounter was that the king's knight lost its head, to the great delight of William. The king held out another to him. But at this moment the boy saw through a slit in the tent one of his own mother's serving-men. He had crept up to spy and listen and find out what was happening to William, for his mother was afraid of the hurt that might be done him. William was overjoyed to see him, and called out, caring nothing who might hear him: 'Welcome, friend Willikin! Tell me who sent you hither! How is my lady-mother and my sisters and brothers?' The man slunk back out of sight and took to his heels rapidly up a narrow cart-track. The king heard William's cry of delight and asked him to whom he was speaking. He said: 'By the faith I owe my father, he was one of my mother's servants; he looked at me through that chink yonder.' 'And why did he not come in by the door?' said the king. They searched for him, but he could not be found anywhere.

I expect the servant took back good news to Lady Sibille, William's mother. Still, she must have been full of joy when finally her little boy was returned to her safe and sound. As you know, the sons of knights usually went to school in the households of great lords, where they learnt all the things a good knight should know. So, when William was about 13, he was sent off across the sea to the Castle of Tancarville in Normandy, where his father's cousin, William, Lord of Tancarville promised to educate him. There he learnt all the proper things and became a good squire to his lord. He had a huge appetite, he sang troubadour songs of love and war, and he said very little. Perhaps his fellow squires envied him, for he was a favourite with their lord and he was very beautiful. This is what the poem says about him:

> His body was so well formed that if it had been fashioned by a *sculptor*, it would not have had such beautiful limbs. He had very beautiful hands and feet, but these were minor details. If anyone looked at him carefully, he seemed so well and straightly made that one would be forced to say he had the best-formed body in the world. He had brown hair. His face even more than his body was fit to be that of the Emperor of Rome. He had as long legs and as good a height as a gentleman could have.

The ambition of every young squire, of course, was to be knighted. But for a long time young William remained a squire, attending his lord at tournaments and in battle, looking after his horses and his armour, guarding his prisoners, but never allowed to fight himself and win glory. At last, in 1167, when the Lord of Tancarville was out fighting for his king, Henry II, he thought the moment had come to knight William. So there and then, in the war-camp and therefore without much ceremony, William Marshal, dressed in a new cloak, was dubbed knight by his lord and girded with his sword. He was so anxious to be in the front of the battle that the first time they met the enemy after this, he dashed forward and had to be called back to let more experienced knights ride out first. All the same, he soon managed to get in the forefront again. A Flemish soldier caught his shoulder with a great iron hook and dragged him off his horse in the midst of the enemy. He managed to get free of the hook and cut his way back to safety, but he had lost his horse. This was serious, for William was poor and could not afford another expensive war-horse. He sold the rich cloak in which he had been knighted and scraped up enough money to buy a baggage-horse to carry his armour, but when news came to Tancarville of a great tournament to be held at Le Mans, William was sad, where everyone else was full of glee, because he could not ride into a tournament on an old baggage-horse. Finally, however, his lord gave him a splendid new war-horse, fast and strong. With the other young men of the castle, William spent a busy night polishing his armour and weapons and at daybreak they all rode gaily away. The tournament was a big one in which 40 knights fought at the same time on each side. William was determined to get a horse for himself! He rushed at a lord, captured him and made him promise to pay a ransom. Then he went back again and captured two more knights! Altogether he did very well for himself: he gained fame as a good fighter and he got lots of booty—war-horses, baggage-horses, palfreys, armour and so on.

Knights at a Tournament

William decided that going to tournaments was an exciting sport. He asked permission to go to another. In the first onslaught he handled his lance so skilfully that he unhorsed one of his opponents, but before he could capture him he was attacked by five other knights. He drew his sword and smote all round him, but one of his opponents hit a great blow at his helmet which turned it right round back to front, so that William could not breathe. He had to retire to his tent to get it off. While he was standing inside, two well-known knights rode past. 'Sir John,' said one, 'who is that knight so clever with his weapons?' 'That is William Marshal,' said the other. 'There is no man more true.' William was so pleased to overhear these words that he got his helmet on again the right way, rode into the tournament once more and fought so splendidly that he won the prize—another fine war-horse.

But life was not all tournaments and games. Sometimes it was bitter warfare and danger. Once with his uncle, Earl Patrick, William was at Lusignan guarding Queen Eleanor, the wife of King Henry II. One day, riding outside the castle all unarmed, the queen and the earl were ambushed and attacked. The earl sent the queen galloping back to safety, but before he could get his armour and prepare for the fight the earl was killed. Young William was hastily sliding into his hauberk when he saw his uncle fall. He was so angry at this treacherous attack that he vaulted on to his horse and charged the enemy without waiting to put on his helmet. The first man he met he cut down with a single sword-stroke. But the next man killed his horse. William quickly disentangled himself and placed his back against a hedge to fight it out single-handed. He kept it up for some time but at last a knight crept up the back of the hedge and, leaning over it, thrust his sword into William's thigh. So William was captured, bound and put on a horse and hurried away by his captors through thick woods and secret places because they feared King Henry's vengeance. No one bound up his wound and he suffered much as they hustled him along. One night, when they were resting in a castle, a lady noticed that the prisoner was wounded. She cut the centre out of a loaf, filled it with flaxen bandages and sent the loaf to William. So, through her kindness, he was able to bind up his wound properly and gradually it healed, though riding night and day with his captors was not good for it. At last Queen Eleanor, who was grateful to the young knight for fighting so fiercely, paid his ransom and gave him rich rewards of armour, horses and splendid clothes, as well as her favour.

William soon won a richer prize still from King Henry and Queen Eleanor. He was made tutor to their eldest son Henry, who was known as the young King Henry. William's task was to teach him to handle his lance and sword, to train him as a good knight should be trained, and to guard him in tournament and battle. He was the captain of the young Henry's company of household knights. William won his young master's favour so much that when the time came for the prince to be knighted, he chose his own tutor, William Marshal, to gird on his sword and dub him knight.

It must have been exciting to live in Henry's household. They were all young men together looking for adventure. Once young King Henry was in rebellion against old King Henry and William had to choose which of his masters he would follow. He decided that his first loyalty was to his young master, but he probably did not approve of the rebellion and was glad when it was over. A great deal of their time was spent in France riding round to places where tournaments were held. William had a glutton for tournaments and, when Henry was tired of them, he would ask permission to go off on his own to some. Some of their adventures were quite comical. One day in a fight young Henry and William got separated from their company of knights and found themselves having to charge 300 French foot-soldiers all by themselves. The infantry were frightened of the galloping horses and just let them ride untouched right through the middle of them. But as they thundered through, William seized the reins of the leader's horse (for he alone was mounted) and dragged him along with them, capturing him right under the nose of the 300 soldiers! They rode swiftly towards their own camp, but, as they went, a low-hanging pipe swept the captive Frenchman right off his horse. William was in front, leading the horse, and had no idea he had lost his prisoner. Henry following behind, saw it all and chuckled, but said nothing. When they

Blacksmiths working on armour

reached the camp, William turned round in triumph to hand over his prisoner to his squire, and behold, he had only a riderless horse! Everyone roared with laughter at the sight of his face, and so did William when he heard how he had lost his prisoner.

At one tournament William received so many blows on his helmet that it was beaten out of shape so that he could not get it off again. At the feast which followed the tournament one of the ladies sent a present of a large *pike* to the knight who had fought most worthily. They decided to present it to William Marshal, but when they went to look for him, they found him kneeling in the blacksmith's shop with his head on the anvil, while the blacksmith hammered away to get his helmet off! It must have been very uncomfortable and everyone felt he deserved the prize. Once, on a tour of tournaments which William and another knight did, they captured and ransomed 103 knights in ten months!

Here is the story of a tournament at Joigni which is told in the poem about William:

Fame, flying swiftly, brought news of a tournament planned by noble barons of high *renown* at Joigni, and to it went all who loved the calling of arms. The Marshal and his company sped so well that they arrived outside the castle of Joigni in good time and dismounted in a pleasant and delightful spot outside it. There they waited while the knights inside armed themselves and then rode out. Then the Countess came forth, who was in both face and person, as I have heard tell, as proper as nature could *fashion* her, and with her were ladies and *damsels* so adorned and so fair that their beauty was beyond reproach, nor had they anything to learn about *courtesy*. The Marshal's knights sallied forth to meet them and felt themselves the better men for the arrival of the ladies. Then, while they waited for more knights to arrive, someone suggested: 'Let us have a dance while we are waiting here—it will pass the time more agreeably.' So they all took hands. Then someone asked: 'Who will sing for us?' The Marshal, who sang well though he never boasted of anything, began a song in a sweetly-tuned voice. It greatly pleased all who were present and they joined in the chorus with a will. When his song, which had given them great pleasure and delight, was finished, a minstrel struck up another song. I do not know what it was about, but the chorus ran:

Marshal, I pray,
Give me a noble horse this day!

When the Marshal heard it, he stayed no longer where he was, but quitted the dance without a word. A squire led up his horse and he beckoned to the little minstrel who ran after him as hard as his legs would carry him. Now some *jousters* were coming up for the tournament. The Marshal, without wasting time in argument, went for one of them with such confidence in his prowess and in the stoutness of his lance that, without more do, he sent him flying out of the saddle. Then he made the little minstrel mount, and he burst right into the dance, crying to everyone: 'See this horse! The Marshal has given it to me!' And everyone was amazed, for they had thought he was still dancing, and there was a great deal of talk about it. The knights and ladies and damsels all said that it was the finest exploit that had ever been performed in any tournament.

William Marshal's service to his young king ended suddenly and tragically when Henry fell ill. As he was dying, he was troubled because he had taken a vow to go on Crusade and fight for the Holy Land and now he would never do it. Turning to William, he said: 'Marshal, you have always been faithful and loyal. I leave you my cross and pray you to carry it for me to the Holy Sepulchre at Jerusalem.' So, when William had taken the body of his young master in solemn and sad procession to Rouen and seen him buried, he set out for Jerusalem, carrying Henry's cloak with the red cross on it. He was away two years, but the poem does not tell us anything about his adventures nor how many Saracens he killed.

When he returned, his gay, adventurous days were over. The old King Henry made him one of his councillors, gave him lands and promised that he should marry a rich heiress. He had to settle down to help with the work of government. But in two years the old king himself died and then William was in a very awkward position. The new king was Henry's son, Richard Coeur de Lion. But only a short while before he had been rebelling against his father and William, fighting loyally for King Henry, had attacked Richard and had actually killed his horse under him. William's friends now shook their heads and said that Richard would revenge himself on the Marshal. But William said calmly: 'Ever since I was made a knight God, in His great mercy, has cared for me so well that I trust in Him for the future.' When Richard sent for William he said: 'Marshal, the other day you wanted to kill me.' William said: 'Sire, I had no intention of killing you, nor have I ever tried to do so. I am still strong enough to direct my lance. If I had wished, I could have struck your body, but I meant only to slay your horse and I am not in the least sorry for that.' Richard said: 'Marshal, I pardon you.' He liked William's frank and courageous words and he knew what a faithful knight he had been in the service of his father, the old Henry, and his brother, the young Henry.

So William became the loyal servant of Richard, who gave him one of the richest heiresses in England for a wife. She was Isabel de Clare, and she owned lands scattered all over England. The centre of her possession was that great castle of Striguil on the river Wye at Chepstow which had first been built by William Fitz-Osbern. She also brought to William, Pembroke, with its strong

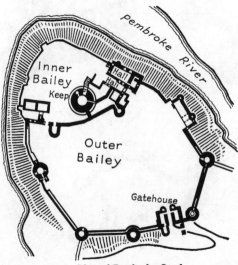

Plan of Pembroke Castle

castle, and many lands in Ireland which had been conquered by her father, Richard (called Strongbow because of his castle of Striguil). Now William had to attend to the business of governing and defending his lands, instead of going to tournaments. He made Pembroke a magnificently strong castle. You remember that it was placed on a cliff sticking out into the mouth of the river. William fortified the highest part of the cliff with a strong curtain wall and ditch. This was the inner bailey in which he built two

Pembroke Castle from the air

halls and a tremendous round keep which was four stories high and had walls averaging 15 ft. in thickness. There was no ground-floor entrance at all and to enter the keep you climbed a stone staircase to the first floor. But between the stair and the door there was a gap with a drawbridge. From the first floor a spiral stair in the wall led down and up to all floors. This was a keep built to be strong, not to live in comfortably.

While King Richard was away on his Crusade to the Holy Land, William Marshal served him loyally at home and tried to prevent the king's enemies from becoming too strong. This meant that he even had to fight Prince John, Richard's younger brother, who rebelled against him when Richard was captured on his way home from the Crusade and thrown into prison in Germany. William worked faithfully to help collect the large sum of money demanded for Richard's ransom, and when the king finally returned to England Richard greeted William as one of the most loyal men.

Although now getting middle-aged, William could still fight well and climb siege-ladders fast. One day, when Richard was making war against the French king, they came to the castle of Beauvais to besiege it. Richard's men placed ladders against the walls and swarmed up them, but the garrison defended themselves so well that one ladder was thrown right down with all the knights on it and the besiegers were driven off the others. A Flemish knight, named Guy, who had reached the top of a ladder, was caught round his neck by a great fork and held there. William was standing on the edge of the moat, directing the attack. He saw the knight's danger and, leaping into the moat instantly, he climbed the opposite bank and then the ladder, sword in hand. He attacked those who were holding Guy so fiercely that they fled. Then his men, seeing William in triumph on the wall, cheered loudly, crying: 'The castle is taken! To his aid!' and rushed up the ladders again. Meanwhile, the constable of the castle attacked William, but with one mighty blow William cut right through his helmet and he fell down like one dead. By this time William was beginning to feel a little tired. He thought he had done his bit, so he sat down calmly on his prisoner and waited until the English had finished capturing the castle. When it was over King Richard said to him: 'Sir Marshal, it is not fitting for a man of your rank to risk yourself in such exploits. Leave them to young knights!' William was fifty-three then, but I think he enjoyed showing them that he could still go up a ladder with all his armour on.

William Marshal grew middle-aged and then old in the service of his kings. After the old Henry and the young Henry, he served King Richard and then King John and, finally, John's nine-year-old son when he became King Henry III. He fought their battles, he besieged their enemies in their castles, he gave them good counsel and he was always loyal. King John made him Earl of Pembroke on the day of his coronation and, although he did not always like the things William said to him, he could not do without this true servant. William, on his side, certainly did not approve of all King John did, but his idea of loyalty meant that he would never rebel against his liege lord. So he would not join the barons' side when they forced John to agree to Magna Carta. Yet he believed in the promises of good government which John made in Magna Carta and once Magna Carta had been sealed, he determined to see that it was kept. William was seventy-two years old when John died suddenly and a great problem arose. Who should rule in the name of the little boy who could not rule for himself? It must be the most true, firm and wise of the barons, and, after anxious thought, they all agreed that this was William Marshal. William said he was too old and feeble and suggested Ranulf, Earl of Chester. But Ranulf said: 'No, Marshal, that cannot be. You are so good a knight, so fine a man, so feared, so loved and so wise, that you are thought to be one of the first knights in the world. I say to you in all loyalty that you must be chosen.' Once William was persuaded that this was his duty, he swore to serve the little king to the uttermost. He said: 'If all should abandon the king except me, do you know what I would do? I would carry him on my shoulders, now here, now there, from isle to isle, from land to land, and I would never fail him even if I were forced to beg my bread.'

So, when he was an old man, William Marshal became Regent of

England. It was a dangerous time, for the French Prince Louis was invading the country and many barons were in revolt. William succeeded in his task. At the end of three years, he had turned the invaders out, beaten the king's enemies, recaptured his castles and brought back peace to the land. In 1219 he knew he could serve no more. He resigned the office of Regent and went to his manor of Caversham, by the river Thames, where he prepared to die. His faithful servant and friend, John D'Erley was there (besides all his family) and it was D'Erley who told the end of the story to the troubadour who wrote the poem. So this is how the troubadour ended his great poem about William the Marshal:

On the day after he had resigned the Regency, it was the Marshal's good pleasure to summon before him all his household. 'Sirs,' he said, 'God be thanked, I may well exult whether it be for life or for death I am now quit of a heavy burden. It would be well that I should complete my last will and testament and that I should make provision for my soul, for the body is in *jeopardy* and I would do well to *disencumber* myself of all earthly things and turn my thought to things of heaven. So he made his arrangements. 'My lord,' said his son, 'We wonder much as to where you wish to be buried.' Then William gave directions for his funeral and for his burial in the Temple. He told his son to give food, drink, clothes and shoes to a hundred poor people on the day of his funeral.

One day his five daughters came in to see him. The earl was surrounded by his knights. William said: 'It is an extraordinary thing: I don't know why it is but I have a great desire to sing.' John D'Erley advised him to try—it might bring back his appetite. 'Be silent,' said William. 'It would not do me any good and everyone would think I was crazy.' Then someone said: 'Sire, call your daughters, that they may sing and comfort you.' So the Lady Matilda sang a verse of a song in a simple, sweet voice. When Jeanne's turn came, she sang a verse very timidly. William gently reproved her: 'Do not have a shamefaced air when you sing; that is not the way to become a good singer.' Then he showed her how to sing. When the girls had finished singing, their father dismissed them: 'Daughters, I pray God to guard you.'

The Marshal again sent for his retainers and the Countess (his wife) and his family. To the Countess he said: 'My dear love, you must kiss me now, since it will be for the last time.' She came forward and kissed him; he wept and she wept, and all the noble retainers who were

73

present wept likewise for very love and compassion. His daughters made great *lamentation* for his sake and none could comfort them. It was necessary to lead the Countess and her daughters from the room, for none could console them. All were weeping and sorrowful.

His sons and a great number of his household kept watch. John d'Erley said: 'My lord, what would you wish to have done with your gowns and furs?' A certain cleric, Philip, spoke up loudly and said: 'My lord, there are many splendid gowns of scarlet with new trimmings of grey squirrel fur, and many other furs, handsome and unworn. You could sell them to buy the absolution of your sins.' 'Be silent, wretch,' said the Earl, 'Never will I follow your advice. Your *ignoble* words trouble me deeply. Soon it will be Whitsuntide and I know well that my knights have a right to the gift of a gown, the last gowns they will ever receive from me. Come hither, John D'Erley, I bid you, by the faith you owe to me and to God that you go and give away these gowns to my knights. If there are not enough, send to London for more.' To his son he said: 'Fair son, I beg you to say farewell in my name to all who have served me well. Thank them in good faith, and may they have thanks from Almighty God alike for their words and deeds.' So the gowns were distributed and when they were shared out, there was not a knight of his household who did not receive one.

Figure of William Marshal on his tomb

Thus died the Marshal, and since he was noble in death as in life, we trust that he is among the saved with God. And so ends the story of the Earl Marshal, which ought to be loved and enjoyed in every place where it is heard.

Investing a Knight

74

The Siege of the Chateau-Gaillard

If you had asked William the Marshal to name the most famous castle in the world, he would probably have said the Chateau-Gaillard. This means the Saucy Castle. 'Chateau', as I expect you know, is the French word for castle and this was, in fact, a French castle, though it was built by an English king. It stood on a bend of the river Seine, high on a chalk cliff, barring the road between Paris and Rouen. The whole of Normandy, with Rouen as its capital, belonged then to the English kings because they were also dukes of Normandy. But the French kings of this time were always scheming to win back Normandy from the English. Richard Coeur de Lion knew this. He had seen many fine fortifications whilst away on the Crusade and when he returned he was determined to save Normandy by building the most splendid castle possible. He started planning and building it in 1197 and it was finished in one year.

Richard I from his seal

You must imagine what it looked like.

The castle itself towered above the Seine on a narrow chalk ridge called the Rock of Andeli. Immediately below it was the new town of Andeli, built and fortified by King Richard. Out in the middle of the river was an island, the Ile d'Andeli, with a palace and tower on it and walls all round. On the north side of the castle the small river Gambon flowed into the Seine through a lake and the old town of Andeli was on its right bank. There were bridges linking the island and the two towns which were both walled. Everywhere, at the gates and at the bridges, the place bristled with towers and

The Chateau-Gaillard

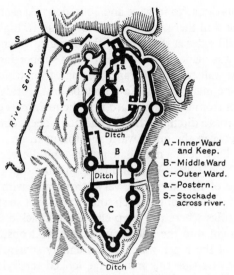

Plan of Chateau-Gaillard

battlements from which archers could shoot. Southwards, towards Paris, there was a stockade right across the deep and swirling river. Everyone marvelled that Richard's engineers could do this, but the greatest marvel was the Saucy Castle itself on top of the Rock.

King Richard himself directed its building, living the while in the palace on the island. Look at the plan of the Chateau-Gaillard. Notice the shape. Everywhere there are curves and rounded towers. Do you remember the weakness of straight, rectangular castles—that it was difficult for the besiegers to hit the enemy when he got right under the walls? Any part of the walls which could not be kept under fire by the garrison was called a 'dead' piece. In the Chateau-Gaillard there were no dead pieces of wall. South-eastwards, towards Paris, the ridge sloped gradually down, so this was the weakest point. You will see at once that this was also the direction from which the French enemy was expected, so here Richard built the thickest and strongest fortifications, in an outer ward (or bailey) shaped like a triangle. Outside this there was a tremendous ditch, 30 ft. wide and 40 ft. deep. At each of the three angles of the wall there was a round tower, 40 ft. high with 11-ft. thick walls. The one at the point of the triangle, which was nearest the enemy, was made even stronger by two supporting towers and a bend in the walls which gave an extra angle from which to shoot at attackers. The main gate had a portcullis and a bridge across the ditch. To get from this outer ward into the main part of the castle, you had to cross a ditch, 30 ft. wide and 20 ft. deep, cut right across the ridge between the outer ward and the next, or middle ward. There must have been a main gate into the middle ward, but we do not know where it was. All round this ward the wall curved along the top edge of the steep hill, very strong and with two drum-towers along the edge of the ditch southwards, not so strong on the other three sides where the steep cliff made attack difficult.

Once you got into the middle ward, the next obstacle was the fortification of the inner ward. To an enemy struggling up from the south or east side this must have looked terrifyingly strong. Across a ditch with a 20-ft. drop he saw a curved wall 30 ft. high. If you look at the plan you will see that this wall is shaped rather like a human ear. On the east and south sides there were rounded *buttresses* jutting out from it, only 3 ft. apart. From these buttresses every part of the wall could be covered by the defenders' fire. The north stretch of wall above the steepest part of the rock was less strongly fortified and here there was a postern gate reached only by a movable ladder. Otherwise the only entry into the inner ward was through a gate defended by two portcullises on the east side.

The final defence of the castle was the keep in the north-west corner of the inner ward. Look at its curious shape—a circle with one sharp point sticking out towards the south-east. This was the strongest point for defending the keep, with walls 18 ft. thick. Inside there was a basement and a first floor in which the only windows looked northwards. Can you think why? The whole base of the keep sloped outwards. I leave you to think out the reasons for this too. All round the inner side of the keep (not on the cliff side) there were extra stone ribs running from the top downwards for some way. These were hollow, so that standing on the top of the wall you could hurl *missiles* on the enemy below down through the slit. These slits are called *machicolations*. Round the top of the keep ran a rampart walk and inside this there rose up two smaller towers, one above the other, rather like a three-tier wedding cake. Standing on the very top a castle watchman could look straight down the steep north slope into the river Gambon as it flowed into the Seine. Turning westward, he would look down at the new town of Andeli and the broad Seine with its fortified island. Turning south-east, he would see the castle defences gradually dropping down the ridge towards the road to Paris. Along that road he would strain his eyes for the glitter of armies approaching. But so long as the Saucy Castle stood, Normandy was safe and the King of England could snap his fingers at the King of France.

Perhaps King Richard believed that the Chateau-Gaillard would defy the French king for ever. But he died in 1199 and his brother John became king. Philip Augustus, King of France, immediately began to plan the attack on Normandy and in the summer of 1203 his army came up the left bank of the Seine and camped opposite the castle. The garrison on the island at once broke the bridges so that the French army could not get over that way. So the French tackled the stockade across the river instead. Although the island garrison was raining arrows and stones on them, a few daring young Frenchmen plunged into the river and chopped a gap in the stockade wide enough for boats to come through. Then Philip Augustus brought up a fleet of flat-bottomed boats, built a bridge across and got his army over the Seine right under the Chateau-Gaillard.

King John had been hovering about at a safe distance without doing much to save his precious castle, but at this point he really tried. He sent William the Marshal to make a night attack on the French camp while a fleet of boats was to creep up the river to break the French bridge and carry food to the castle garrison. There was a confused battle in the darkness, first in the camp and then on the river. While arrows, stones, boiling oil and pitch rained on them, the boatmen tried to break the bridge. At last a great oak beam fell on two of the biggest boats and sank them. The rest rowed away as fast as they could and the land attack was beaten off as well. Next the French attacked the island garrison. So long as the wooden palisade all round the island held, the garrison could stand out. At last a young Frenchman, Gaubert of Mantes, tied a rope round his waist and swam out with a potful of burning charcoal which he threw against the palisade. Instantly it caught fire and the flames swept right over the island, burning many soldiers and forcing the rest to surrender.

But still the greatest obstacle, the great castle itself, towered above the besiegers. It looked impregnable; all the French could do was to dig trenches, build wooden huts for themselves, and settle down to a hard winter trying to starve the garrison out. The castellan, Roger de Lacy, had enough food to last his fighting garrison for as long as a year, but a great many of the townsfolk from Andeli, perhaps 1,400 of them, had fled for refuge into the castle. These were useless mouths just eating up the food and Roger realized that he had made a great mistake in letting them in. Across the ditches the French soldiers jeered and sang a mocking song: 'The nest is overcrowded with nestlings who will have to turn out when the spring comes.' Alas! they had to be turned out in the hard winter. Roger made up his mind he must get rid of them. First he pushed out the oldest and weakest and they were allowed to go through the enemy army unharmed. But when the rest were driven out of the castle, to their horror the French drove them back again with showers of arrows. They rushed back to the castle to find the gate barred against them. So the poor wretches were forced to seek shelter in the holes and cracks of the rock between the two armies, with no protection from the cold winter and no food except dead dogs. It was three months before Philip Augustus relented and allowed them to be fed and then only half were still alive.

Meantime the French prowled round the castle looking for weak spots. At last Philip Augustus decided he must try a direct attack on the point of the triangular outer ward. Between the round tower at that point and his army there was, you remember, the deepest and widest ditch. To protect his soldiers Philip had a

80

covered wooden passage built right up to the edge of the ditch. Through it the French carried a wooden tower on wheels which they set up on the edge of the ditch. From this cross-bowmen shot with deadly fire among the soldiers defending the wall. Meanwhile others were busy carrying earth and anything they could find through the passage to tip into the ditch. They got impatient, however, long before it was filled up, so they brought scaling ladders and scrambled down into the ditch. Climbing up the other side the ladders were too short but, in spite of a rain of arrows and stones, many struggled up, using swords and daggers as pointed sticks to help them. Once underneath the wall, some held shields up to keep off the shower of missiles, while the sappers dug away as fast as they could at the tower's foundations and laid a mine. At last they managed to blow up a big piece of the tower and Roger de Lacy only just had time to get his men across the drawbridge into the middle ward before the French came pouring through the gap into the outer ward.

So one step was gained. But the next looked just as bad: another wide, deep ditch and strong wall with no easy way of attacking it. But, prowling along the edge of the ditch, a young soldier named Bogis (or Snub-nose) saw a little window just above the wall, belonging to a new building put up by King John. Together with a few friends, he scrambled down into the ditch, climbed up under the window and then, by standing on a friend's shoulders, Bogis could just get in through the window. It was unguarded! He sprang inside, let down a rope to his friends, and they all climbed in. Then they found they were locked inside a building! They hammered on the door and shouted. The garrison, realizing that some French soldiers had got in, set fire to the building. Unfortunately the wind caught the fire so that it swept all through the middle ward. The garrison fled into the inner ward, their last refuge, but miraculously Bogis and his friends escaped. They rushed out and, when the fire had died down, opened the gate and let down the drawbridge. So the French captured the middle ward.

Now in the inner ward there were 180 of the garrison left. They might have held out still but that in this last defence there was one great weakness. This ward, like the others, was defended by a ditch and a wall, but leading up to the gate on the east side there was a fixed bridge of rock over the ditch, instead of a movable drawbridge. Over this bridge the French brought a 'cat', which was a sort of tent on wheels with men inside it who began at once to undermine the gate. Then they brought up a heavy mangonel which shot huge stones at the gate. At the third shot the undermined wall suddenly fell and the French poured into the inner ward. Roger had no time to get his men into their final stronghold of the keep. They were surrounded and captured at once. So, on 6 March 1204, after a six-months' siege, the Chateau-Gaillard fell to Philip Augustus, King of France. On that day King John of England really lost Normandy, for nobody could have conquered it so long as the Saucy Castle stood.

Besiegers using a 'cat' and besieged throwing stones, etc., on them

Larger and Grander Castles

In most of the castles we have been talking about the keep was the most important part. It might be a shell-keep on a motte or a four-sided great tower or one of the newer circular towers, but as a keep it was the central stronghold. No besiegers had captured the castle until they had stormed it, while the defenders knew they always had a sporting chance of holding out if they could retreat to the keep and defend it. That is why so many of these keeps had staircase entrances with turns in them, or a drawbridge in front of the doorway on the first floor, or special windows and doors from which the defenders could shoot down at enemies coming up the stairs. But in the hundred years after Henry II, the end of the twelfth and the beginning of the thirteenth century, some changes took place in castle-building. First, they wanted more space inside the castle grounds, so they built large outer baileys with curtain walls and sometimes moats round them. Secondly, the old keep became much less important and the castle-builders concentrated on bigger and stronger walls, with more towers along them and elaborate gatehouses. Thirdly, castle-dwellers more and more found the stone keeps, built to be strong fortresses, uncomfortable to live in, so they built elegant halls with chambers and kitchens attached, generally along the curtain wall of the inner bailey. As we have seen, some barons did this much earlier, but now it became the usual custom.

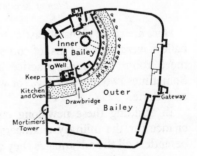

Plan of Ludlow Castle

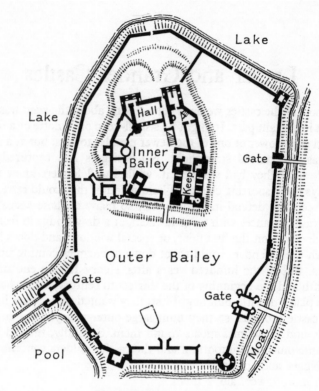

Plan of Kenilworth Castle

Here are some plans of castles to show you how these large outer baileys were added. This, of course, gave the castle-dwellers much more room for horse-practice and for holding tournaments. Sometimes two more baileys (or wards) were built, as at Chepstow and Corfe.

In building these new long curtain walls there was plenty of chance for the military engineers to use their wits in giving the defenders all the advantages they could. The most important thing was to give them as many chances as possible to shoot down the enemy trying to climb the walls. If you have a straight wall, only

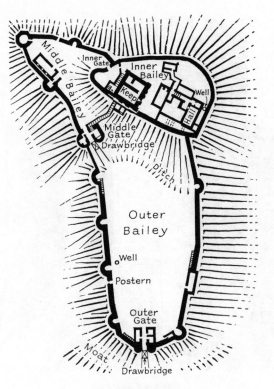

Plan of Corfe Castle

one or two archers at a time can shoot down from the top of it on to the same spot below. If you have projecting towers, or flanking towers, at intervals along the wall, you can shoot at the same spot from several angles, as you can see from the piece of Conway Castle wall on the next page.

Of course some castles had projecting towers before this, but often these were haphazardly placed. Now it became common to build curtains with towers placed regularly along them, usually round or polygonal, not square. Do you remember the reason for giving up square towers?

Conway Castle wall

The most important point to strengthen was, of course, the gate-house and this became much more elaborate than ever before. In the first place, it would be flanked by towers so that the besiegers would be caught in the narrow space between. You can see this clearly in the picture of Rockingham Gatehouse on the next page. The actual entrance was by a narrow passage through the gate-house itself with all kinds of defences in it. Now imagine what it would be like to try to force your way through a strong thirteenth-century gatehouse. Look at the plan of Warkworth Gatehouse on the next page.

Rockingham Gatehouse

First, you would have to cross the moat when the long drawbridge was raised, and when you had scrambled up to the gate, you would

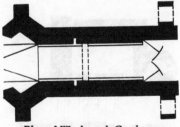

Plan of Warkworth Gatehouse

be in the direct fire from the tower arrow loops on either side. Then you must force your way through a gate which opened outwards. Inside, you were in a narrow passage between the gate and the portcullis and here the defenders could shoot at you through loops from the guard-rooms on either side of the passage. Next you faced the heavy iron portcullis which was let down by machinery on the first floor above the gate. On the other side of the portcullis was one of the nice little traps invented to deal with besiegers. It was just a long, narrow slot in the roof or arch above the passage through which the defenders on the first floor could shoot down on the besiegers as they pushed through the gatehouse. Do you remember that these slots were called machicolations? All the way along the passage you would be under fire from the cross-arrow-loops on either side, until finally you came to one more gate which you had to break down before you were inside the castle. It was quite a business storming such a gatehouse!

As time went on the castle engineers made the defences of the gatehouse more and more elaborate. They often put in several machicolations, both on the outside and on the inside of the portcullis, and sometimes two or more portcullises. Look carefully at this plan of Pembroke Gatehouse and imagine what the difficulties of getting in would be. Pembroke gatehouse had an extra last defence which you can see in the picture opposite, taken from inside the castle. Do you see the arch between the two towers? As the besiegers came

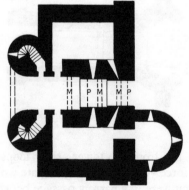

P.— Portcullis
M.— Machicolation

Plan of Pembroke Gatehouse

Pembroke Gatehouse from the inside

rushing into the bailey, thinking they had finally finished with the gatehouse, the defenders could shoot at them from the rear, for the arch is really a concealed gallery.

The next thing the castle-builders did was to make it more difficult to get up to the gate quickly by building a fortification outside the gate, called a *barbican*. This was sometimes a small, walled court, and sometimes just two strong walls which narrowed the approach and squashed the besieging men into a small space where they could easily be shot at from the walls of the barbican or the gatehouse itself.

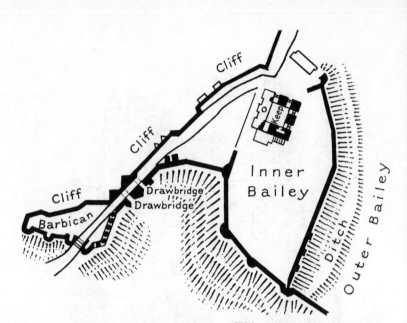

This plan of Scarborough Castle shows a walled barbican narrowing to the drawbridge. This picture of Warwick Castle shows you the barbican which was a narrow passage.

Sometimes the passage was made still more of a death-trap by a right-angled turn at the end.

The engineers grew more cunning about everything. You might not think that there was much skill in cutting an arrow-loop—just a slit in the wall through which to shoot! The problem was how to keep the archer hidden and protected from the besiegers and yet to

90

give him good elbow-room and make it possible for him to shoot outwards at an angle as well as straight in front of him. So even the simplest arrow-loops were slots which were widened out (or splayed) inside, to form a place for the archer, sometimes with a seat. Then they began to think of ways in which to increase the archer's range of fire. First, they cut away the stone at the foot of the loop outside, so that he could more easily shoot straight down below him at an attacker trying to scale the wall. Then they widened this base still more, making a triangular foot to the loop. Then they experimented with cross-slits, to give the archer a wider side range of fire, and finally they put larger round holes in the loops. But all the time they kept the actual opening so narrow that an attacker from outside would have to be a very good shot indeed to put an arrow straight through the loop. Look at this row of different arrow-loops and you will see how they gradually developed:

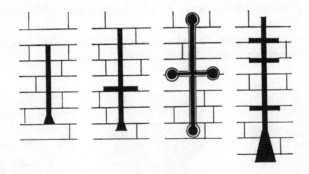

If you were going to defend the curtain properly, there must be a good wall-walk all round the top of it, just as the Norman castle-builder had built one all round the keep. To shelter the guards walking round you needed a good parapet at least six feet high, but if this was of solid stone the guards could not see out easily, and, worse still, could not shoot at besiegers. This was the problem. It was solved by building the kind of parapet or battlements we call *crenellated*, as in the picture on the next page. The solid pieces of

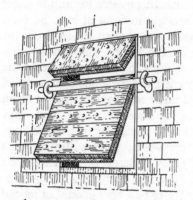

stone were called *merlons* and the openings *embrasures*. As the guards passed the embrasures, they were, of course, exposed to enemy shooting, so, to meet this danger, they often put wooden shutters across the embrasures, like this:

Perhaps the greatest problem in defending the curtain was how to get at besiegers who had managed to creep close up under it and were trying to weaken or sap the foundations of the wall or even to mine right underneath it. The defenders needed to be able to shoot or to throw such unpleasant stuff as quick-lime straight down below them. We have seen how they designed the arrow-loops to meet this difficulty. Another answer was to build battlements with machicolations all round.

Yet another idea was to make wooden galleries, called hoardings, which jutted out right round the top of the wall.

Crenellation   *Hoarding*   *Machicolation*

Of course, as defenders thought up better ways of strengthening castles, so besiegers invented better siege-engines. The battle of wits went on. Many kings and barons went on crusades and brought back home with them new ideas about castle-building. One was the idea of having two or three rings of defending walls instead of one very strong keep in the middle. We call these *concentric* fortifications. At the end of the thirteenth century there was a great castle-building king in England, Edward I. He had actually been on a crusade and seen some marvellous fortifications, so it is not surprising that, after he had conquered Wales, he should have

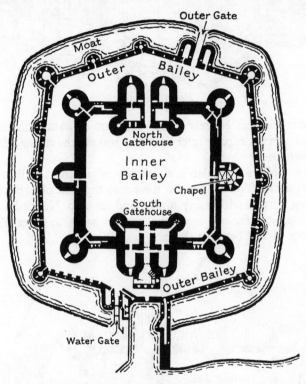

Plan of Beaumaris Castle

built some wonderful castles of the new pattern. Here is the plan of Beaumaris Castle on the Isle of Anglesey just off the coast of north Wales. See how many differences you can find between this and a Norman castle.

Did you notice that there was no keep at all, or a motte, and that

Beaumaris Castle

the defences were entirely in the two lines of walls with strong, round towers at regular intervals? Did you see the strong, elaborate gatehouses?

Now look at this plan and picture of another of Edward's famous castles. You will see that it is not on the same plan, but it has a strong curtain with many towers and no keep. Notice how the towers project far out from the curtain so as to cover all the stretches of wall between them.

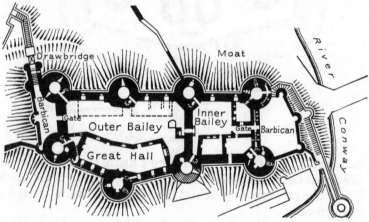

Plan of Conway Castle

The old keep was given up not only as a last fortress of defence, but also as a place to live in. The later, elegant halls, were built not for strength but for beauty and comfort. They had large windows, proper fireplaces with chimneys, better kitchens and comfortable private chambers for the lord and his family.

The castles of Edward I's reign were very different from the little motte-and-bailey ones which the first Normans built so

Conway Castle

quickly. They were much bigger and grander and looked much more like the castles we imagine to ourselves than those grim, plain tower keeps which belong to the twelfth century. They were more elegant and comfortable to live in. Were they more useful? The first castles had served the Normans very well as strongholds when they were conquerors in the midst of an angry and resentful people who might rebel at any moment. In the twelfth century barons' castles had often been a nuisance to the king, but they were very useful to their owners. Do you remember how often the besiegers failed to capture the castles, so that the lord, safe inside, could snap his fingers at the enemy? The king's own castles were also exceedingly useful to him, especially on the Welsh and Scottish borders and those defending his lands in France. Do you remember that John did not lose Normandy until the King of France had managed to capture his famous castle of Chateau-Gaillard? In those days kings fought each other more often by besieging each other's castles than by fighting pitched battles.

But all the time ways of fighting were changing, just as they have changed in this present century. The trench warfare of World War I was quite out of date by World War II. So in the fourteenth century castles began to go out of date. This was partly because the siege engines got too good and could smash the walls too easily, and partly because fighting battles became more important and war-captains discovered that archers were even better used on the battle-field than sniping from castle walls. When Edward I built his grand castles, he did not know they were going out of date, though perhaps he had an inkling by the end of his life, for he never finished Beaumaris Castle. Soon men began to see that in most wars castles were no longer very important, though occasionally one might suddenly be very important for a moment.

Perhaps these later castles were very pleasant to live in, but they were no longer really useful. Perhaps, if you had been a boy or girl living in a fourteenth-century castle, you might secretly have wished you were back in the exciting days of the twelfth century, when the castle defenders were always ready for the besiegers who might appear any day.

Grey Mare's Tower, Warkworth Castle, showing elaborate arrow loops

96

HOW DO WE KNOW?

In finding out about castles the main thing to study is the castles themselves. By excavation we can often discover where the first castle stood on a site and how it was altered and enlarged until it grew into the latest castle standing there. People expert in knowledge of castles can often tell the dates of castle-building by the way the walls are constructed; they can also tell us why castle-builders built certain special things, e.g. traps for attackers. Thus, even from the buildings themselves, we can discover some of the thoughts of castle-builders. Then there are records, especially records kept by kings, which tell us exactly when certain castles were built or altered or repaired and how much money was spent on them. King Henry II was particularly good at leaving us this kind of record. Finally, when we want to find out how people lived in castles, we read stories and poems which they themselves wrote about knightly adventures, about tournaments, about besieging castles and even about falling in love. The story of the siege of the Chateau-Gaillard was written for us by William the Breton who saw it all. We can also see knights besieging castles in some of the pictures drawn by monks in the manuscripts which they wrote. Above all, we are lucky to have a long poem about the famous knight, William the Marshal. At the end of his long life he told many of his exciting adventures to one of his faithful servants and these were made into a French poem by a troubadour. In this book I have given you a few of these adventures translated into English. In reading history it is a wonderful thing when we can get close to people who lived centuries ago, as we can to William the Marshal in this poem.

THINGS TO DO

IN A GROUP

1. Make a map of your own county marking all the castles you can discover. Remember to show how they are placed, e.g. by a river or on a high point.

2. Make a set of models or pictures to show the development of English castles from the simple Norman motte-and-bailey castle to Edward I's great Welsh castles. You will find plans and pictures to help you right through this book.

3. Make models to show the different methods and engines used in besieging a castle.

4. Write and act a play about William the Marshal's adventures as a little boy.

5. Make a model of a tournament such as William the Marshal attended.

6. Make a model of the Chateau-Gaillard from the plan and picture in this book.

7. Make a Book of Castles.

BY YOURSELF

1. Make a list of all the French words to do with castles which you can find in this book. Why did castle-builders in English use so many words which came from the French?

2. Visit, if possible, one of the famous castles and make your own plan and drawings of it. You could do this for a class book of castles.

3. Imagine yourself one of the garrison of Exeter Castle. Write a diary of the siege by King Stephen.

4. Draw pictures of the following scenes:

    The Scots prince dangling outside Ludlow Castle (p. 31).

    Robert FitzHubert climbing into Devizes Castle with his men (p. 32).

    Queen Matilda escaping from Oxford Castle (p. 33).

5. Draw a picture, or make a model, of a twelfth-century knight in armour and name the various pieces of armour.

6. Write a story or a poem about a twelfth-century knight and his lady.

7. Make a set of pictures showing the whole story of the siege of the Chateau-Gaillard.

8. Write an account of the life of William the Marshal, as it might have been written by one of his servants.

9. Write an essay explaining, with diagrams to make your meaning clear, exactly how later castle-builders improved the defences of castles.

GLOSSARY

armourer : one who looks after armour

armoury : place where armour is stored

bailey : castle yard with wall, bank or moat, or all three round it

ballad : story in verse meant to be sung

ballista : machine for shooting stones

barbican : outer defences protecting castle gate

battering-ram : long, heavy, wooden beam with iron head for breaking down walls and gates

battlements : walk on top of castle walls protected by parapet

beleaguered : besieged

boar : wild pig

bower : private room for lady

breach : gap or hole in wall

buttress : extra stone support to strengthen wall

butts : targets for archers

castellan : keeper of a castle

charger : large, heavy war-horse

chausses : chain-mail armour for legs

chevron : zigzag pattern used in carving stone

chronicler : writer of a chronicle or history

coat of arms : special badge belonging to one family

concentric : built in rings, one inside another

conical : shaped like a cone

courteous : possessing *courtesy* or good manners

crenellated : parapet made with alternate higher and lower sections

curtain : wall round castle bailey

damsel : young girl

to disencumber yourself : to get rid of something which is a nuisance

distraught : upset

to divert : to amuse

dowry : money or land given by a father to a daughter when she marries

drum-tower : round tower

embrasure : opening in parapet on top of castle wall

falconer : man who looks after *falcons,* or hawks

to fashion : to make

fletcher : man who makes arrows

foray : raid

fortification : walls, banks or ditches to fortify a castle or make it strong

gambeson : padded leather tunic worn under hauberk

garderobe : lavatory

grappling-iron : big iron hook used to capture prisoners

hauberk : shirt of linked iron rings (ring-mail or chain-mail)

hide : leather

honour : lands owned by a baron

hostage : person handed over to an enemy as a pledge that promises will be kept

ignoble : mean

impregnable : impossible to capture

inaccessible : impossible to reach

javelin : short spear meant to be thrown

jeopardy: danger

jouster : knight who takes part in *jousts* or tournaments

keep : chief and strongest tower of a castle

lamentation : weeping

lance : spear

loop : narrow slit-window

machicolation : slit in battlements through which to attack enemies below

mangonel : engine for throwing large stones

merlon : solid bit of castle parapet alternating with gaps (embrasures)

missile : any weapon thrown at an enemy

motte : mound

oath of fealty : solemn promise to be faithful

palfrey : small horse for a lady

palisade : wooden fence

pavilion : tent

pewter : metal, mixture of tin and lead

pike : big fish
polygonal : having more sides than four
portcullis : spiked gate which can be raised and lowered from above
postern : small gate
quarry : victim to be hunted down
quintain : stand with two arms for practising tilting
rampart : walk on top of bank or wall
rectangular : with four corners
renown : fame
sconce : holder for torch
sculptor : carver in stone
shaft : handle
shell-keep : round tower with open space inside
solar : private room for the lord's family
splayed : sloping
steward : man who manages the lord's affairs
stockade : wooden fence
strategic point : strong position
surcoat : linen tunic worn over hauberk
tankard : metal mug for drinking
tilting-yard : yard in which knights *tilt* or practise for tournaments
tournament : mock battle in which knights practised fighting
troubadour : singer
truce : peace made between two enemies for a little while
vassal : man who has sworn an oath of fealty to a lord

SOME INTERESTING CASTLES TO VISIT IN
ENGLAND AND WALES

Berkshire
Windsor

Cambridgeshire
Cambridge

Cornwall
Launceston
Restormel
St. Michael's Mount
Trematon

Cumberland
Carlisle
Cockermouth

Derbyshire
Peveril

Devonshire
Dartmouth
Lydford
Totnes

Dorset
Corfe
Sherborne

Durham
Barnard Castle
Durham
Lumley
Raby

Essex
Colchester

Hedingham
Ongar
Pleshey

Gloucestershire
Berkeley

Lydney

Hampshire
Christchurch
Odiham
Portchester
Winchester

Herefordshire
Clifford
Ewias Harold
Goodrich
Hereford
Longtown Wigmore

Hertfordshire
Berkhampstead

Isle of Wight
Carisbrooke

Kent
Allington
Chilham
Dover
Leeds Castle
Rochester

Saltwood
Tonbridge

Lancashire
Clitheroe
Lancaster

Leicestershire
Ashby de la Zouch
Belvoir

Lincoln
Lincoln
Tattershall

London
Tower of London

Monmouthshire
Caerleon
Caldicot
Chepstow
Grosmont
Monmouth
Raglan
Skenfrith

Nottinghamshire
Newark
Nottingham

Norfolk
Castle Acre
Castle Rising
Norwich
Thetford

Northamptonshire
Rockingham

Northumberland
Alnwick
Bamburgh
Lindisfarne
Newcastle
Norham
Tynemouth
Warkworth

Oxfordshire
Broughton
Deddington
Oxford
Shirburn

Shropshire
Acton Burnell
Bridgnorth
Clun
Ludlow
Shrewsbury

Somerset
Dunster
Farleigh Hungerford
Nunney

Staffordshire
Dudley
Tamworth
Tutbury

Suffolk
Bungay
Burgh
Clare
Framlingham
Orford

Surrey
  Farnham
  Guildford

Sussex
  Arundel
  Bramber
  Bodiam
  Hastings
  Lewes
  Pevensey

Warwickshire
  Brinklow
  Kenilworth
  Warwick

Westmorland
  Appleby
  Brough
  Brougham

Wiltshire
  Old Sarum (Salisbury)

Yorkshire
  Bolton
  Conisbrough
  Helmsley
  Knaresborough
  Middleham
  Pickering
  Pontefract
  Richmond

  Scarborough
  Tickhill
  York

Wales
  Beaumaris
  Caerphilly
  Cardiff
  Cardigan
  Carew
  Carmarthen
  Caernarvon
  Castell Coch
  Chirk
  Cilgerran
  Coity
  Conway
  Criccieth
  Denbigh
  Dolbadarn
  Ewloe
  Flint
  Harlech
  Kidwelly
  Llanstephan
  Manorbier
  Montgomery
  Ogmore
  Pembroke
  Rhuddlan
  Tretower

Then and There Filmstrips

The Medieval World
A boxed set of three filmstrips with notes
suitable for pupils working on their own,
or for teachers. The strips provide original
source material mostly in colour, which is
complementary to the medieval Then and
There titles.

Filmstrip 1 Royalty, Knights, Castles,
Tournaments, Religious Life
Filmstrip 2 Country Life, Sports and Pastimes
Filmstrip 3 Town Life, Home Life Travel

ISBN 0 582 24115 4